MW01621059

Looking Back at Vermont

Looking Back at Vermont

FARM SECURITY ADMINISTRATION PHOTOGRAPHS, 1936–1942

Nancy Price Graff

Middlebury College Museum of Art · Middlebury, Vermont

DISTRIBUTED BY UNIVERSITY PRESS OF NEW ENGLAND

HANOVER AND LONDON

This catalogue accompanies the exhibition *Looking Back at Vermont: Farm Security Administration Photographs, 1936–1942,* on view at the Middlebury College Museum of Art, September 12 through December 1, 2002.

Published by Middlebury College Museum of Art, Middlebury, Vermont

Distributed by University Press of New England, One Court Street, Lebanon, NH 03766

LIBRARY OF CONGRESS CONTROL NUMBER: 2002111156

ISBN 1-928825-02-8

Edited by Norma Roberts
Managed by Douglas Perkins

Book design and typography by Christopher Kuntze
Composed in Utopia and Ellington types
Printed by Balding + Mansell Limited, Norwich, England

Contents

PREFACE

This volume, *Looking Back at Vermont*, accompanies an exhibition of the same title. The project has been the occasion for Guest Curator Nancy Price Graff (Middlebury Class of 1975) to chronicle the largely untold story of what drew a small group of government photographers to Vermont during the years 1936 to 1942. Over the past few decades this story has been overshadowed by the travels of some of the same photographers to other parts of the United States. Through Graff's efforts, however, the particular patterns of their Vermont travels are made clear, as well as the reasons for their selection of specific subjects.

This is a fascinating history and it helps to give greater meaning to these varied and occasionally ambiguous photographs. Some images bring to mind the cliché that these were "simpler times" that we may be inclined to romanticize. Others, however, quickly remind us that for many Vermonters life during these years was physically arduous and that, at the end of the day, the material rewards might well have been meager.

We hope that this revealing account will help readers to see the period more accurately and that it may also provide them with an appreciation for the varied works of the Farm Security Administration photographers who have left us this rich photographic history.

Richard Saunders
DIRECTOR
MIDDLEBURY COLLEGE MUSEUM OF ART

ACKNOWLEDGMENTS

Many people contributed to bringing this project to fruition and these remarkable photographs to the public eye. My thanks go to Marjorie Zunder, Diane Wishinki, and the other staff at the Vermont State Library, who arranged for an extended loan of Roy Stryker's papers on microfilm from the Archives of American Art and generally helped me track down many loose ends. I would also like to thank Michael Taylor and Scott Lovelette, at the Kellogg-Hubbard Library in Montpelier, who processed my interlibrary loan requests. I am grateful, too, to the staff of the Vermont Historical Society Library.

My thanks go to many people at the Middlebury College Museum of Art: Margaret Wallace, who attended to numerous details; Anthony Lewis, who read the manuscript and offered useful and perceptive comment; Emmie Donadio, who as acting director of the museum during the 2000–2001 academic year took a turn overseeing the project; Douglas Perkins, who was brilliant and indefatigable in tracking down the images for this publication and exhibition; Ken Pohlman, whose expertise in designing the exhibition was critical; Norma Roberts, my editor; and Christopher Kuntze, with whom I was delighted to work once again.

The passage of time between the six-year period when Historical Section photographers were busy in Vermont and the present made it difficult to locate people who were personally familiar with the section's assignments, but I am grateful to Conrad Ormsbee and Marilyn Ormsbee Piro for sharing their memories, their mother's diary, and the Fritz Henle photograph that remains in their family's collection. In addition, I thank the staff of the Library of Congress Prints and Photographs Division, who helped me with my research in Washington; Donna Whitcomb, assistant town clerk in Eden, Vermont, who researched the history of Roy Stryker's cottage on Lake Eden; and Robert Howrigan, of Fairfield, who supplied details about the Gaynor family, the object of Jack Delano's attention in 1941.

Special thanks are due to Louise Rosskam, who consented to several telephone interviews about her work in Vermont during the summer of 1940. Her recollections of her work and the general atmosphere of the Historical Section contributed significantly to this project. I am pleased that this publication will be the first to credit her with photographs that were long mistakenly attributed in the Library of Congress archives to her husband.

Richard Hathaway generously read the manuscript with a critical eye toward how this work fits within a study of Vermont. Of course, if any errors remain, they are mine alone.

St. Lawrence University has been generous enough to lend a color print, one of only a handful of color photographs taken of Vermont during the summer of 1941 by Jack Delano.

I would like to thank my husband, Chris, and my children, Garrett and Lindsay, both of whom virtually lived with this project through much of their teens. They tolerated my enthusiasm and listened attentively to my monologues about these extraordinary photographs without ever seeing more than a handful of images. I hope that this publication will finally give them a sense of the work with which I have been engaged.

Finally, I owe a debt larger than I can ever repay to Richard Saunders, director of the Middlebury College Museum of Art, whose vision, patience, good humor, and determination kept this project moving forward despite numerous obstacles. Six years ago, when I was casting about for a project, he handed me six reels of microfilmed Historical Section photographs of Vermont and asked me to look at them and tell him what I thought. Richard, thank you; this is what I think.

Nancy Price Graff

GUEST CURATOR

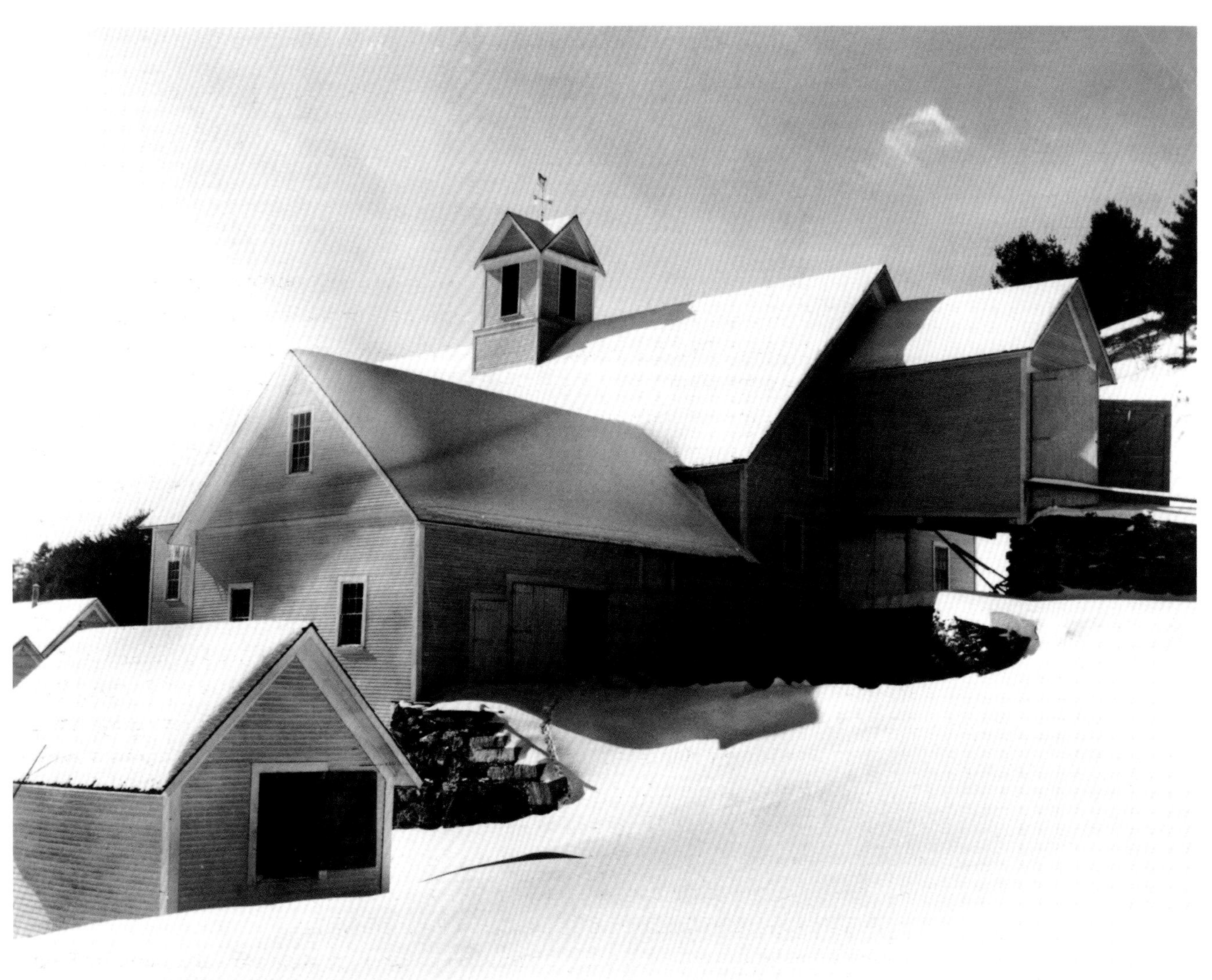

FIGURE 1

Arthur Rothstein

Windsor County, Vt. February 1936. Barn of a dairy farmer.

Looking Back at Vermont

FARM SECURITY ADMINISTRATION PHOTOGRAPHS, 1936–1942

Nancy Price Graff

On 31 January 1936 Arthur Rothstein, a twenty-year-old photographer with the U.S. government's Historical Section, then under the Resettlement Administration, left Washington, D.C., in his car, headed for northern New Hampshire. His assignment was to take pictures of winter recreation activities and pulp mill operations—what his boss called "the cooperative lumber industry"—in some of the depressed communities that formed a buffer between central New England and the Canadian border.[1] These images were intended to show bureaucrats in Washington, and any other interested Americans, how one of the poorer regions of the country was coping with the Great Depression by relying on traditional uses of its natural resources. Years later, Rothstein complained that the snow and cold weather made the work technically some of the most difficult he ever faced.

Although Rothstein's assignment would largely confine him to New Hampshire, he arrived first in Windsor, Vermont, on 5 February at 7:30 P.M., having driven up that day from New Haven, Connecticut. The next day he spent taking pictures in Windsor County. By 8 A.M. on 7 February he was on his way to Lancaster, New Hampshire.[2] The photographs that he would take in New Hampshire over the coming week would be work. In Vermont, however, Rothstein had freer rein. Apparently 6 February was clear and cold. The photographs he took of farms blanketed in snow are rich with the brilliant contrast of sunlight and shadow. In one spectacular photograph, a parade of attached barns and outbuildings climbs a hill, the stark, geometric mosaic of dark roofs and vertical planes a counterpoint to the bright, soft, unbroken field of snow that surrounds them (fig. 1).[3]

For more than sixty years, approximately a dozen photographs that survive from Rothstein's 1936 visit to Vermont have been largely lost to anyone looking for Vermont views. They remain misfiled in Washington, D.C., at the Library of Congress, under the heading, "Windsor County, New Hampshire," although no such place exists. Nonetheless, they are among the hundreds of thousands of photographs on file that were taken by the staff of the Historical Section during the later years of the depression and up to and including the outbreak of World War II.

Rothstein's visit to Vermont opened the door in the state to one of the most extraordinary federal government projects ever undertaken. Between the winter of 1936 and the autumn of 1942, nine different photographers made a total of eleven visits to Vermont on behalf of the Historical Section, first under the auspices of the Resettlement Administration, later under the Farm Security Administration, and finally under the Office of War Information. Altogether, they spent only a small amount of time in the state. Typically they were on the road taking photographs in all forty-eight states, and their periods in Vermont were usually sandwiched between other assignments. They were, strictly speaking, government employees who were being paid to document the plight of rural Americans and the success of New Deal programs in addressing their needs. However, that original mandate was absorbed over time by expanding goals. What began as a relatively modest intention to serve the public relations needs of controversial government programs blossomed through the vision of Roy Stryker, a passionate and inexhaustible director, into the most sweeping cultural history project ever undertaken by the U.S. government. Before the Historical Section was disbanded at the outbreak of World War II, these photographers and a handful of others contributed more than a quarter of a million negatives to an extant archive that captures the United States in a delicate balance, emerging from the waning years of the depression and poised on the cusp of the economic and technological transformation generated by World War II.

Approximately 1,600 negatives of Vermont taken as part of this government program survive in the national archive at the Library of Congress. This collection shows Vermonters at play, at county fairs, working their fields, ironing clothes, making paper, quarrying stone, bottling milk at dairy cooperatives, exercising their democratic privileges at town meeting, sugaring, skiing, putting their children to bed, and salvaging steel for the war effort. It also captures the breathtaking beauty of the land and the heartbreaking details of the state's poverty. It is an unparalleled document of Vermont emerging not just from the Great Depression but from a century of hardship dating back to 1840, when a discouraging number of Vermonters began pulling up stakes and moving westward hoping to find better fortune. Indeed, some of the photographs could have been taken in 1840 rather than 1940; others capture the despair of generations of Vermonters who struggled to endure in many corners of the state while the nation's prosperity passed them by. Hundreds of other photographs, however, portray the state at its finest, peopled by decent, modest, hard-working Vermonters, the kind around whom myths gather like moths to a light.

The Vermont images constitute an almost minuscule proportion of the total number of photographs taken by employees of the Historical Section, but numbers do not tell the whole story. No single Vermont image ever achieved the iconic status of Dorothea Lange's *Migrant Mother,* to name one of the Historical Section's most famous photographers and photographs. Nonetheless, the state played a special part in the project. For one thing, its director, Roy Stryker, had a summer home in Eden Mills, Eden, in the northern part of the state, and this is where he came to rest and think about his project's direction. He did not always find peace. More than once while he was vacationing in Vermont, a crisis arose compelling him to jump a night train back to Washington. The cottage also became a popular and convenient stopover for photographers making their way around Vermont.

Thanks to Stryker's cottage in Vermont and his willingness to share his experience and his home with the photographers who worked under him, we have pictures of some of the residents of Eden taken over the span of several years, something that was normally precluded by the peripatetic nature of the photographers' work. In addition, Stryker himself accompanied at least one photographer during a working swing through the state, a collaboration that was unusual between staff photographers accustomed to working alone and a director who rarely meddled with the actual field work. Finally, Stryker's obvious affection for Vermont influenced how he saw the state and how it was portrayed in this vast photographic document, and, perhaps even more important, how those photographs were used at the time to portray Vermont to the rest of the nation.

NOTES

1 / Roy Stryker to George Gercke, 12 February 1936. Gercke, based in New Haven, Connecticut, was Regional Information Advisor for the Resettlement Administration.

2 / Rothstein, travel voucher, February 1936. Library of Congress.

3 / Figure captions appear as they did on the original prints. These captions sometimes differ from those now appearing on the Library of Congress website.

A Brief History of the Historical Section

As the 1920s ended, 1,700,000 farms in the United States earned an annual gross income of less than $600. Nearly half these farms grossed less than $400 annually, and more than half of those grossed under $250 annually. Almost eight million rural Americans were so destitute that even the poverty line was a nearly invisible horizon too distant to be gained.[1] Technology was alleviating the crisis, but it was also contributing to it. According to one analysis of the time, twenty-two tractors and twenty-three four-row cultivators could displace 130 sharecropping families leaving them without marketable skills, income, or homes.[2] Displacement was an especially acute problem in the South and Southwest, where approximately seventy-five percent of the farmers were tenants.[3] The nation's farmers were frightened and confused. In pushing for higher tariffs earlier in the decade in the hope of staving off the foreign competition that bloomed in the adolescent world economy after World War I, they had unwittingly sowed for themselves a bitter harvest. Most other legislative initiatives designed to aid farmers did not survive the decade's Republican administrations; those that passed tried chiefly to aid farmers indirectly by encouraging money to trickle down from the hands of exporters and businesses into the threadbare pockets of the rural poor.

The Farm Security Administration was neither the first nor the most influential government program created to address the plight of rural Americans in the early 1930s. When Franklin D. Roosevelt was sworn in as president in 1933, he inherited a nation so desperate for agricultural reform that a majority of normally conservative farmers was eager to accept any plan that offered relief. Nearly helpless individually, they were clamoring for government intervention on a national scale.

The Agricultural Adjustment Administration was an early invention of Roosevelt's New Deal. Very simply, the plan provided government price supports to farmers but required reciprocal reductions in crops. One of the AAA's chief proponents was Rexford Guy Tugwell, assistant secretary of agriculture and former professor of economics at Columbia University. During the late spring of 1934, Tugwell recruited Roy Stryker, an economics instructor from Columbia with whom he had collaborated on several projects and at least one book, to take a temporary, summer position in the Information Division of the AAA in Washington.

History turned on this appointment. Roy Stryker was a short, nervous, energetic Westerner with a bullish temperament much like Theodore Roosevelt's and interests similarly broad. Born into a populist, socially active ranching family in Colorado, he eventually came East to New York City to study at Columbia University, and took a job, with his wife, Alice, at the Union Settlement House. At Columbia, Stryker came under Tugwell's spell. Like Harry Carmen in the university's history department and John Coss in the economics and government department, Tugwell believed in teaching abstract subjects visually. They were drawn to field trips and an emerging line of textbooks, such as Yale University's Pageant of America series, which employed maps and photographs of buildings, activities, people, and commerce to illustrate their subjects. Stryker was fascinated. He completed his bachelor's degree and stayed on to pursue a master's degree, during which time Tugwell asked him to collaborate on a new book that he and others were compiling for an innovative course at the university titled "Contemporary Civilization." Stryker's job was to collect, sort, and select illustrations for the new book.

Stryker found his work at Columbia consuming and deeply satisfying. By day he led economics students on field trips to Wall Street, banks, slums, and wharves to introduce them to the ways an intangible economy manifests itself. By night he assembled several thousand visual images—photographs, etchings, maps, and graphs—and pored over them to select the best illustrations for the new textbook, which was eventually published in 1925 as *American Economic Life and the Means of Its Improvement.* Stryker became fascinated by his discovery that while photographs could illustrate abstract social problems and economic theories, few publishers took advantage of this opportunity. Furthermore, most magazines of the era used photographs to distort American life, either by presenting idealized images, like Edward Steichen's fashion photography, or art, like Edward Weston's or Alfred Stieglitz's landscapes.

Another revelation came as Stryker discovered the photography of Mathew Brady, Jacob Riis, and Lewis Hine. Here were photographers dating back almost a century who had trained their lenses on the nation's social issues and produced photographs that shocked a nation with an unfiltered look at the horrors of war, aroused sympathy for New York's homeless, and provoked outrage over children forced to work in factories. Moreover, as Stryker was quick to realize, these photographs had a powerful aesthetic quality to them. Their composition, use of light and shadow, their clarity and subtle tonal values enabled them to stand on their own as art.

The first edition of *American Economic Life* was barely off the presses before Stryker began work on a second edition, which was published in 1930. By that time Stryker had been promoted to instructor in economics. The later book reflects the increasing sophistication Stryker demanded of photography and the illustrations he chose. He included considerably fewer photographs culled from commercial agencies, and instead selected growing numbers of images taken by photographers such as Lewis Hine and the young Margaret Bourke-White. The technical quality of the work, combined with the photographers' acute sensitivity to the social issues of the Reform Era, resonated in the visually inclined economics instructor and unintentionally gave him the perfect introduction to the work that lay ahead.

By the time Stryker arrived in Washington in the early summer of 1934, the idea that photography could combine high technical standards, aesthetics, and a social conscience was firmly planted in his mind. His job description at the AAA was vague enough to give him some latitude in his work: "to plan, execute, and advise with regard to informational material in the form of charts, graphics, and other pictorial and visual media, relating to the programs and activities of the AAA."[4] It was no great jump, therefore, for Stryker to suggest that the AAA publish a heavily illustrated book about American agriculture using photographs chosen from the Department of Agriculture's extensive archive, but it was probably only because Tugwell was assistant secretary of agriculture that the idea was not shelved in favor of something that appeared to benefit the American farmer more directly.

Indeed, Tugwell loved the idea. Stryker worked throughout the summer of 1934 and continued after he returned to Columbia to teach in the fall. In the spring he hired one of his former students, senior Arthur Rothstein, a founder of the Columbia University Photography Club and already an accomplished photographer. To Rothstein fell the tiresome work of duplicating and standardizing photographs that would illustrate the book.

In the end, the book was not published. Instead, Stryker returned to Washington during the summer of 1935 for another three months. Following Tugwell as his work evolved under the New Deal, Stryker took a job in the newly created Resettlement Administration under his mentor, who had now been appointed the first director of the agency. Although the RA was designed to address the needs of the poorest one-third of American farmers, few of whom had benefited from the price supports engineered by the AAA, the new agency was controversial from its creation. One of its mandates was to improve the lot of farmers, particularly tenant farmers struggling to survive on marginal or sub-marginal land. The RA sought to accomplish this in several ways: by providing low-interest loans that would enable farmers to move to better land; by rebuilding eroded and depleted soil; and by offering a variety of other programs to improve rural life, one of which involved moving unemployed city families to small towns where they might outlast the depression with a small garden plot and a part-time job.

Tugwell anticipated that these programs would have the potential both to help and to disturb great numbers of Americans. Consequently, he created an Information Division within the RA to act as a publicist for the agency. He chose Stryker for a job within the administration precisely for his protégé's experience in using photographs to promote social and economic ideas. However, Tugwell also chose Stryker for his energy and enthusiasm. A passionate communicator in the classroom and in his books, Stryker was asked to address an entire nation, and to do so using not words—which were being employed by the government in mind-numbing numbers—but photographs, specifically the kind that would evoke a visceral and immediate sympathy for the Americans who needed help the most.

Stryker's title, "Chief of the Historical Section of the Information Division," provided a poor description of his duties. Although he was being asked to create an agency archive to record the RA's efforts and successes, he was also specifically charged with directing "the activities of investigators, photographers, economists, sociologists and statisticians engaged in the accumulation and compilation of reports, . . . statistics, photographic material, vital statistics, agricultural surveys, maps and sketches necessary to make accurate descriptions of the various . . . phases of the Resettlement Administration."[5] The implication is that he had a large, trained staff at his disposal to accomplish these ends, but the truth was that he had no staff and no clear direction. While waiting impatiently for the economists, investigators, and sociologists to appear, he hired Arthur Rothstein and put him to work photographing the RA's paperwork in order to have thorough records. The specialists never arrived, and soon all the Historical Section had was a growing collection of photographs.

The idea of photographing a government agency's efforts and accomplishments was novel and appealing. Photography units sprouted in other divisions within the RA and indeed throughout many branches of the federal government. Soon the system, or lack of one, became unwieldy and wasteful, and Stryker was able to convince Tugwell to consolidate all RA photography within the Historical Section. The effect was threefold: it created a critical mass of work large enough to make photography an important part of the RA's work; it gave Stryker's Historical Section a focus it had heretofore lacked; and it persuaded Stryker to give up teaching in favor of staying in Washington to oversee work that increasingly intrigued him.

In the end, although the Historical Section was never specifically designated a photography division, it became exclusively that. Rothstein helped Stryker set up a modern darkroom. Stryker also found competent staff to work in the lab and acquired two more photographers. Carl Mydans, who had been hired in another division within the RA, was transferred to the Historical Section. Walker Evans arrived highly recommended after doing part-time work for the Department of the Interior. Stryker welcomed both men; he knew of Mydans's experimental work with 35mm cameras, and he knew of Evans's growing reputation as a visual artist with a conscience. Evans, who would go on to become the best-known photographer in the Historical Section, had, in particular, a profound influence on almost all of the section's photographers who followed. He brought with him an approach to photography that elevated the medium from a mechanical process to an indisputable art. His painstaking compositions, his insistence on using unsophisticated equipment, and his refusal to crop his images or manipulate them in the darkroom all set a standard for an aesthetic that most of the succeeding Historical Section photographers would try to emulate. Moreover, both Evans and Mydans arrived at a time when Stryker's ideas concerning the role that photography could play in the national dialogue were still evolving, and the expertise and talent of the two photographers did much to shape their new boss's aesthetics and goals.

Two other artists also had a profound effect on Stryker's vision. The first was Ben Shahn, who was not a professional photographer, but a painter hired within the Special Skills Division to help design the interiors of RA offices. However, in his travels Shahn occasionally wielded a camera to capture scenes that he might later paint on his return to Washington. Over time his portfolio grew to include hundreds of photographs, and Stryker was so taken by the artist's arresting images of a devastated land and a destitute people, images both visually stunning and emotionally wrenching, that he asked to have Shahn's collection incorporated into the Historical Section's fledgling archive. The collection was especially significant because Shahn used it to confirm Stryker's faith in the power of photographs as propaganda. Before then, the didactic power of the image was still a matter of abstract debate. However, Stryker emerged from dozens of long discussions with Shahn convinced that photographs could convey to the American people the extent of the tragedy of the nation's rural poor and thereby persuade growing numbers of suburban and urban Americans to support the extensive government programs needed to lift their fellow citizens out of poverty. Stryker felt, in short, that if Americans could see with their own eyes the extent of the crushing devastation their hearts would open their minds and wallets.

The other artist whose work influenced Stryker was Dorothea Lange. Lange was a young photographer from California whose technically perfect photography, as artistically realized as Steiglitz's, was informed by a passion for social justice. Her ability to confront human misery in ways that captured the viewer's eye and heart first came to Stryker's attention in a report published by the California State Relief Administration, and he hired her without having met her. For six months before she traveled to Washington to meet Stryker, she sent East a relentless stream of heartbreaking photographs of migrant farm workers, and, even without her presence, the work was powerful enough to articulate her sympathy for her subjects and her vision of socially conscious photography.

The photographic mission of the RA grew not from any grand design but from these inspired exchanges among some of the leading photographers of the time, from Stryker's creative interpretation of the section's official charge, and from an expedient effort to consolidate the far-reaching branches of an unwieldy new government agency. By the start of 1936, the Historical Section had an up-to-date darkroom and five photographers: Evans, Mydans, Rothstein, Lange, and Theodore Jung (who stayed fewer than six months). Just as important, Roy Stryker was awakening to the possibility that the photographs gathering in his office could be the documents against which the American people could assess the nation's current condition and direction. And the public was taking note. A week before Christmas in 1935, the *Washington Daily News* explained to the public the purpose of this burgeoning government archive:

> The photographs, officials believe, will present more forcibly than could any printed words the problems with which the New Deal and Resettlement Administration are wrestling—the problem of bringing a modicum of comfort, health and happiness to the men and women who have been sucked to the bottom of our social structure.[6]

On 1 September 1937 the U.S. Department of Agriculture took control of the RA and changed its name to the Farm Security Administration. Tugwell resigned, leaving Stryker without his friend in high places who had protected and nurtured the Historical Section as it competed with every other New Deal initiative for the government's limited dollars. The change did not alter the Historical Section's assignment. However, it did force Stryker to take a more active role with Congress, and in the months and years ahead he spent considerable time at the Capitol trying to save the section's budget from those who could not see the benefit of sending photographers on the road at great expense and for months at a time to take pictures.

Stryker spent the rest of his time trying to organize the growing file, as the archive came to be called, and overseeing the posse of photographers working in the field. Although the Historical Section, even in its flushest periods, never employed more than six photographers, those who were employed at any given time were rarely in the office. Their life was on the road (Arthur Rothstein and Marion Post even shared an apartment in Washington because they were never in the city at the same time), and Stryker's connection with them was by letter, occasionally by telegraph, and only rarely by telephone. Letters from the photographers to Stryker were full of information about their experiences in the field, both positive and negative; requests for film and flash; and self-criticism about the work they were putting in the mail. Stryker's to them were long—often ten to twelve handwritten pages—and chatty, covering happenings in the office and the internecine battles of government agencies. He was especially skillful at providing the kind of individual encouragement needed by field photographers who had only their equipment and travel as constants in their lives.

Ever a teacher, Stryker preferred to take care of general education before the photographers left Washington. For instance, before any of them departed on a first assignment, Stryker instructed them to buy a copy of J. Russell Smith's *North America: Its People and the Resources, Development and Prospects of the Continent as the Home of Man*, which he considered to be an encyclopedia of information about different regions of the country.[7] They were to read it carefully and carry it with them. Part economics, part sociology, and mostly geography, *North America* introduced Historical Section photographers to the socioeconomic conditions they would encounter in their travels, and, according to Stryker, would make their eyes sensitive to the complexities and significance of what they were seeing in their viewfinder. In addition, before leaving on an assignment, the photographer was required to sit down with the chief of the Historical Section and broadly discuss a region or a state until Stryker was convinced that he or she had a solid grounding in its history and in how the economic forces at play there affected the local population.

In addition to this verbal briefing, photographers were usually provided with what eventually came to be called a shooting script; that is, a list of possible photographic topics for each locale that would illuminate its socioeconomics. The list might include a specific directive such as to shoot a roadside sign advertising a tourist home, or a broad suggestion to shoot a series illustrating, for example, the process of getting milk from the farm to the creamery. The script also included ideas for both stock pictures and those images that more rightly belong in the category of photojournalism, a new term that Stryker loathed but one that better described the kind of photograph that told an entire story in a single frame. Despite the script, Stryker gave the section's photographers considerable freedom to discover the region in which they found themselves and to use their judgment in choosing the images that would make visible the problems of the rural poor and lead to solutions that might offer them hope. Stryker's letters to the photographers were sprinkled with innumerable inquiries and questions that kept their curiosity alive to the region before them. As soon as the photographs started coming in, Stryker responded by letter with copious criticism, tailoring his letters to each photographer's temperament and trying always to shape the kinds of images he thought would be most useful.

He also wasted no time putting the photographs to work. Fortified by an almost religious zeal that these images transcended propaganda and would be catalysts for necessary change in the country, Stryker embraced the challenge of using photographs to spread word of the RA's work with the rural poor. Toward this end, he wanted to distribute as many of the section's photographs as widely as possible. As a result of successful self-promotion, the section's photographs began to appear regularly in the *New York Times*, the *Washington Post*, the *New York Evening Post*, the *Kansas City Star*, the *New York Herald Tribune*, *Fortune* magazine, and the *St. Louis Post Dispatch*. News services such as the Associated Press and United Press, eager to add graphics to their regional stories about the nation's problems and its relief efforts, distributed Historical Section photographs to large and small newspapers across the country. *Survey Graphic*, a progressive, socially aware magazine that had published the photographs of Dorothea Lange and Lewis Hine even before the Historical Section came into being, welcomed the flood of images that now became available through the government and sometimes used the section's photographs exclusively to illustrate its articles.

As satisfying as this must have been for the chief of the Historical Section, publication also provoked bitter criticism that pained Stryker and raised difficult ethical issues. From the beginning, the publication of government-generated photographs in privately owned newspapers and magazines created a public furor that deterred some from accepting Stryker's handouts. The primary issue was the indiscriminate blending of news and what some viewed as propaganda in ways that made it possible for government photographs to masquerade as journalism. A secondary concern was unease over government meddling with private enterprise. In both instances, and especially early on, many newspapers and magazines circumvented the thorny issues they faced by running the Historical Section photographs without credit lines.[8] These omissions bothered Stryker, but he showed restraint. He protested to the media and apologized to his photographers, but at least during the first few years of the Historical Section's existence, he was willing to tolerate the practice as long as the photographs were being published.

Not surprisingly, Republicans largely ignored the ethical concerns of publishing government-generated photographs and seized on the political implications. They got an early jump in the summer of 1936, when five photographs Arthur Rothstein had taken the previous April near Fargo, North Dakota, were exposed as misrepresentations. Rothstein, in North Dakota to take pictures of the drought, had found a bleached steer skull on a cracked and baked alkali flat. Taken with this desolate image, he included the skull in five photographs, in each one moving it (even onto nearby grass) to change the composition. The photographs were widely distributed through the Associated Press until August, when an enterprising editor in Bismark chose the occasion of one of President Roosevelt's agricultural fact-finding tours of the upper Midwest to publicly question the integrity of artificially composed government photographs. It was a public relations nightmare both for the Democrats and for Stryker, who had to defend his section's work against partisan accusations that Historical Section photographers were little more than New Deal toadies. The issue never died, and from 1936 until 1942 section photographs released to almost any medium faced Republican sniping and second-guessing that grew, in time, as irksome and wearisome to Stryker as a pebble in his shoe.

Even the aesthetics of the Historical Section's images caused problems for Stryker in his efforts to distribute the photographs. Some, such as Dorothea Lange's *Migrant Mother*, Arthur Rothstein's *Dust Storm, Cimarron Co., 1936*, and Russell Lee's *Children Eating Christmas Dinner*, became icons of the national crisis almost as soon as they were released. However, in becoming widely known, they inadvertently set a new standard for mass-media photography that many magazines and newspapers were ill-prepared to match. Chagrined at the inferior quality of their own product, some magazines and newspapers fell back on the practice of using the Historical Section's photographs in their pages but omitting the appropriate credit lines.

The new style of photography was popular not just because the aesthetic of the medium was changing dramatically but also because its technology was evolving, intriguing professionals and making photography more accessible to amateurs. In a letter responding to a query from the editor of *Popular Photography*, Stryker explained that the Historical Section photographers were using Eastman, Leica, Contax, Ikonta (2¼-inch square), Speed Graphic (3¼ × 4¼ inches), and Recomar cameras. Some photographers also had 8 × 10-inch view cameras. Stryker added that many of the photographers were also using Linhofs, but these were not yet government issue.[9] Later, Rothstein and Lee would have an elderly man in Washington, D.C., convert their unwieldy Linhofs into hand-held cameras that could replace their Speed Graphics.[10] Rothstein and Lee also tinkered constantly with the emerging technology of flash photography, trying to improve the synchronicity between flash and shutter movement and the reliability of equipment that all too frequently failed to perform as desired.[11] The movement generally was toward smaller, hand-held cameras, especially after *Life* photographers showed a preference for 35mm cameras that relied on available light.[12] Years later, however, Carl Mydans questioned a common misperception of the times: that the new equipment he and his peers were then helping to introduce to the public assured photographers of better photographs. Talent, he said, was still critically important:

> You don't make better pictures; you work with greater ease, but to think that a better camera and better film gives you better pictures is simply another way of saying that if you gave an artist a better brush and a better grade of canvas he would paint a better picture.[13]

Stryker, who understood little about the mechanics of photography, agreed with Mydans that talent and sensitivity were paramount. When magazine editors pressed him to reveal the mechanical particulars of specific photographs, he grew exasperated and sometimes intentionally provided the wrong f-stop numbers for them to publish, hoping to make his point by embarrassing them.[14]

Americans were changing too. In a letter to Stryker, the publisher of *Graphic Manual* described a possible chapter in a future issue that would evaluate contemporary trends and attempt to articulate the future of photography. "Photography in America is providing a new visual language which is even replacing the symbol of words in many cases," he wrote. "Where more reading knowledge was required in the past, the photography of today has quickened the tempo of learning."[15]

Life (launched in 1936) and *Look* (launched in 1937) were glossy new magazines created to capitalize on this new visual language. Both quickly developed symbiotic relationships with the Historical Section that advanced everyone's interests. Within four months of the publication of the first issue of *Look*, Stryker wrote to Tugwell's secretary: "Incidentally, magazines like *Life* and *Look* are helping our case a lot."[16] The influence of the Historical Section's photographs on the magazines was swift and dramatic, even though many of the section's images were too subtle to be considered for layouts that often crowded half a dozen images on one page. Gardiner Cowles Jr., founder of *Look*, contacted Stryker even before the first issue was published and asked for photographs of "the worst conditions in the South, pictures which might run under the caption 'Can such conditions possibly exist in the United States?'"[17] Two months later, after Stryker had perused the first issue and approved the bold way the magazine ran pictures, he offered *Look* exclusive photographs for future assignments.[18] Perhaps more than any other form of media, these widely successful new photojournals gave Stryker the bully pulpit he sought. Shamelessly using the section's images to promote government intervention on behalf of the rural poor, he worked tirelessly but with a clear conscience, confident that his motives were pure and the goals unassailable.

Nonetheless, at times the interests of the Historical Section and these influential magazines ran counter to each other. The publishers of both magazines were committed to attracting the nation's most talented photographers to their staff at a time when many of them worked for the government. Sometimes this made life difficult for Stryker. *Life* lured Carl Mydans away from the RA in 1936, and in 1940 Arthur Rothstein was lured away by *Look*, where he remained for twenty-five years.

A second significant showplace for the photographs was government publications. At first the Historical Section was necessarily limited to providing images of people and conditions that had not yet been touched by first the RA's and later the FSA's agricultural programs. As time passed, however, the section's photographers were able to document some results of government programs—a farmer who had joined a dairy cooperative, a farm wife who was learning how to feed her family more nutritious meals. This was valuable validation for a young agency trying to prove its worth amid a plethora of programs all competing for funding and attention. Not surprisingly, the RA and then the FSA culled from the Historical Section's increasingly rich file almost every type of image they needed to illustrate pamphlets such as "Resettlement Administration, An Introduction to the Agency's Work"; "America's Land, An Explanation in Laymen's Terms of the Agency's Approach to Land Use"; and "Farm Tenancy—The Remedy: Twenty Questions Asked and Answered." However, the photographs that may have been most important in safeguarding the RA's future appeared in publications such as the *First Annual Report of the Resettlement Administration.* Here members of Congress had the chance to measure for themselves how effectively images supplied by the Historical Section could be combined with text explaining needs and programs.

A third outlet was books. Photographs reproduced in books were probably distributed among smaller audiences than those widely published in newspapers and popular magazines, but books offered a permanence and an opportunity to articulate a larger discussion than that offered by any other medium. Before the era ended, more than a dozen books were published that relied heavily or exclusively on Historical Section photographs, including a 1940 edition of Stryker's bible, *North America.*[19] Two of the best-known books were tangentially, rather than directly, related to the Historical Section, and both featured the work of a single photographer. Undoubtedly the most famous one derived from the section's emerging photographic aesthetic was *Let Us Now Praise Famous Men* by Walker Evans and James Agee. Evans was technically on leave from the RA in 1937 when he took these classic photographs, collaborating with Agee on an article on Southern sharecroppers for *Fortune* magazine. The article was never published, and Evans and Agee then offered their work to book publishers. Several of them also rejected it, however, uncomfortable with its strident tone and its blunt, unapologetic images. The book finally appeared in 1941. By that time war was imminent and the public's sensibilities had been blunted by several years of graphic exposure to the tragedy of Southern poverty, so Evans's and Agee's book, which later sold millions, received only a lukewarm reception. (Although Evans was not working for the Historical Section when he took these photographs, Stryker managed to acquire them for the file.)

Dorothea Lange had a similarly disappointing experience when *American Exodus: A Record of Human Erosion* was published in 1939. Written by her husband, sociologist Paul Taylor, and illustrated exclusively with Lange's photographs, *American Exodus* featured images culled from her work in the section's file. However, in reprinting the negatives, Lange retouched some to make them more aesthetically pleasing to her. Stryker strenuously objected when he learned what she had done, and for this and other reasons Lange and the Historical Section soon parted ways. Although *American Exodus* may have been the most beautiful contemporary published collection of Historical Section photographs, it never attracted the popular success Lange had hoped to achieve.

The first significant book employing a cross-section of Historical Section images and having Stryker's input and blessing evolved from a proposal by Archibald MacLeish. In a letter to Dorothea Lange, Stryker enthusiastically explained that "the general theme is the people left stranded by the outwash of industry in America, industry being used in a broad sense."[20] By the time *Land of the Free* was published in 1938, however, Stryker's opinion of MacLeish's brutally spare poem about the country's dispossessed had cooled. "The book had a rather interesting reception," he wrote to Lange. "The pictures, I would say, came out on top in every case. There seemed to be a divided opinion about whether or not Mr. MacLeish had made a contribution to literature."[21]

A more successful and significant book, Sherwood Anderson's *Home Town* was published in 1940, at about the same time that Richard Wright's *Twelve Million Black Voices* and Arthur Raper's *Sharecroppers* were released. Unlike the latter two, *Home Town* drew exclusively on Historical Section photographs. Combining text and photographs, it used 142 images to comprise a paean to the kind of complex and intimate community life that Anderson believed formed the bedrock of the nation's democracy. The file was full of relevant images manifesting Stryker's interest in small towns. This fascination was piqued by his childhood experiences in Colorado, his work in New York and Washington, and by a critical meeting he had in the spring of 1936 with Robert Lynd, a Columbia University sociologist and author of the pioneering urban study *Middletown*. From that long and animated discussion, Stryker took away the notion of expanding the section's work to include a study of small-town life, with the idea of examining whether families in small towns were subject to the same agents of change that were transforming those in urban settings. By 1937 the questions that Lynd raised for Stryker were influencing shooting scripts and introducing new themes to the file such as the exploration of complex sociological issues about class, power, recreation, domestic life, physical mobility, and even dress. Stryker found it easy to justify this broad theme as the nation witnessed the poignant exodus of Americans from farms to small towns and cities. This tidal demographic shift inevitably changed the communities where these migrants landed as well as the rural areas they left behind.

According to an anonymous description of the place of the small town in the section's work, "The Small Town is the cross-roads where the land meets the city, where the farm meets commerce and industry. It is the contact point where men of the land keep in touch with a civilization based on mass-produced, city-made gadgets, machines, canned movies and canned beef." To underscore how powerfully the theme resonated in the section's work, the author explains that "because of the importance of the Small Town in American rural life, every Farm Security Administration photographer carries a permanent small-town shooting script." Among items on the accompanying sample shooting script were stores, traffic signs, men loafing and talking, women waiting for the men, ice-cream parlors, churches, filling-station attendants, and restaurant life.[22]

Although proposed by Historical Section media coordinator Edwin Rosskam and written by Anderson, *Home Town* gave Stryker an opportunity to showcase the small-town theme. The tone of the book is unabashedly nostalgic, covering the seasons, the characters, and the institutions that are almost universally present in small towns: the spinster schoolteacher, the town drunk, the newspaper, the court as local soap opera, the ebb and flow of commerce, the social intercourse that thrives on front porches everywhere. However, the last section of the book is devoted to a discussion of the impact of the automobile, the growth of mail-order and chain businesses, the ubiquity of radio, all factors that Anderson blamed for undermining the stability of what he considered the nation's most sacred social, economic, and political unit. Anderson does not bemoan the end of the hometown—indeed, Historical Section photographers captured aspects of it in thousands of communities across the country—but he urged that it be protected against modern forces such as an increasingly nationalized culture and the dislocation of people from the land they knew as home. Moreover, he specifically praised the camera's role in spotlighting the strengths of and threats to American hometowns. Calling their photographs "purposeful," Anderson credited the Historical Section's "inclusive attitude which makes photographer, eye and camera into an instrument of social science."[23] Although the book received a mixed reception because of its occasionally insipid tone, Stryker was so taken with it that he wrote to the Historical Section photographers in the field and asked them to contribute to a fund to purchase publicity copies for government officials such as the Secretary of Agriculture and the Secretary of the Treasury.[24]

Publication, however, was not the only way to feature the images accumulating in the ever-expanding file. Once it became clear that taking the photographs met only half the Historical Section's mandate, Stryker began struggling to find venues where the photographs could be publicized. Too busy to attend to it himself, he hired Rosskam to serve as a liaison with publishers, to package articles for organizations and institutions, and to create traveling exhibitions of the photographs. Before the Historical Section folded in 1942, it probably hosted or contributed to hundreds of exhibitions, both to promote the government's interests and to demonstrate the innovative work being done with new camera technologies. Small, general exhibitions of perhaps twenty prints were popular at country gatherings, but modest exhibitions were also organized for libraries, stores, public schools, and union conventions. Sometimes specific exhibitions were developed for relatively select audiences.[25] In 1936 alone, Historical Section photographs were exhibited at the Democratic National Convention, the California Pacific International Exposition in San Diego, the Texas Centennial Exposition in Dallas, and the Great Lakes Exposition in Cleveland.[26] That same year Stryker asked Eleanor Roosevelt to write the foreword for a traveling exhibition of 110 photographs being organized for the College Art Association.[27] Between 1936 and 1942 the section provided photographs for exhibitions at everything from Gimbel's Department Store in Pittsburgh to the Southern Conference for Human Welfare to the 1939–1940 New York World's Fair. The audiences for many of these exhibitions were not large or particularly influential in promoting the FSA's cause, but they became primary venues for reaching urban audiences, and as a result of these shows the Historical Section's style of photography began to be recognized as some of the most innovative art being produced in the country.

The most important exhibition of Historical Section photographs, *How American People Live* premiered as part of the First Annual International Photographic Exposition at the Grand Central Palace in New York City, 18–29 April 1938. One week before the exhibition opened Stryker wrote to James McCamy, who taught in the social studies department at Bennington College in southern Vermont, and explained that the photographs would run large, from 11 × 14 to 30 × 40 inches, and that the theme would be "people—people in various circumstances throughout the United States."[28] The response to the Historical Section photographs was immensely gratifying to the photographers and their boss. According to Stryker, Ben Shahn said that the seventy-six Historical Section prints "didn't give anyone a chance to catch their breath."[29] Several days before the exhibition ended Stryker wrote to Edwin Locke, his assistant, that "it is not exaggerating a bit to [say] that we scooped the show. Even Steichen went to the show in a perfunctory manner, and got a surprise when he ran into our section."[30]

One of the staff photographers, Arthur Rothstein, curious to know how the section's photographs would be received, proposed that a response box accompany the display. Over the course of the ten-day exhibition, close to five hundred visitors wrote down their thoughts after studying these stark photographs of their countrymen and -women. The comments generally reflect the staggering impact of the images: "Without a doubt these pictures are the most human, forceful, and interesting pictures I have seen of the South"; "Let's have more pictures like these, but let's get a sane president so that business can pick up and change such conditions"; "Thank you for this exhibit. It brings home to me some of the things in our country that we need to do something about"; "Propaganda! A select few!"[31] When he heard some of the responses, Rexford Tugwell, Stryker's friend and former boss, suggested that the comments be forwarded directly to President Roosevelt, a suggestion that was as much about publicity for the struggling Historical Section as it was about Tugwell's wish to have the reflections directed where they might influence the president's social policy. To Stryker's further delight, when curators from the Museum of Modern Art, in New York, saw the Grand Central exhibition, they offered to host a tour of Historical Section photographs throughout the country.[32] Soon after, *Documents of America: The Rural Scene*, derived from photographs taken between 1935 and 1938, became one of the Museum of Modern Art's traveling exhibitions, available as a two-week rental for $25.[33]

Although Stryker never referred to the International Photographic Exposition as pivotal in the life of the Historical Section, in some ways it roughly marked the end of one era and the start of another. By 1938 photographers had taken a surprising number of the photographs that would make the Historical Section famous. The country had been severely jolted by certain images that seared their way into the national consciousness, and publications requested these same photographs over and over again until Dorothea Lange disparagingly called them "cookie cutters."[34] What she had in mind was the stereotypical Historical Section photograph: bleak and grim, full of sunken cheeks and blank stares or desiccated land.

Things were changing in several ways, however. Conceived as an instrument of record to assist the RA, the Historical Section had quickly evolved and assumed new responsibilities. By mid-1937 the RA had been renamed the Farm Security Administration by the Bankhead-Jones Tenancy Act and been subsumed by the U.S. Department of Agriculture. The Historical Section's assignment now was to use innovative means to spread awareness of the need for radical social change. The new goal appealed strongly to the section photographers. "I think we had a great social responsibility," Arthur Rothstein said years later. "We were dedicated to the idea that our lives can be improved, that man is the master of his environment, and that it's possible for us to live a better life, not only materially, but spiritually as well."[35]

Even Adolph Hitler played a part in charting the section's evolving course. The grim portrayal of the United States by the early Historical Section photographers may have shocked Americans, but Hitler acquired copies of some of those same images and used them as propaganda to persuade his people that the United States was too broken spiritually and physically to pose a threat to German nationalistic dreams. This appalled Stryker, who reacted to this discovery as if the photographs exposed the nation's soft underbelly, and it planted in him a fierce desire to find strengths to herald. In a general letter to the photographers in the field, he advised them to seek out positive images that would highlight the nation's strengths:

> You will keep this ever in mind: Lots of food, strong husky Americans, machinery, show it as big and powerful, good highways, spaciousness. Also watch for such things as good schools, freedom of education, church services, meetings of all kinds. . . . Watch out for particularly important nationality groups, particularly in the rural areas. Scandinavians, Swiss, Portuguese, Spanish, showing community life, close-ups of people and activities.[36]

Ultimately, however, neither bureaucratic reorganizations nor world events had as great an impact on the evolution of the Historical Section's work as did Roy Stryker's energy and imagination. As early as 1937 images emerged showing that photographers were no longer focusing solely on destitution and despair. Rather, Stryker's dream of compiling a portrait of the United States that surpassed anything ever before attempted steadily expanded the boundaries of the Historical Section's mission. The file became an archive capturing the country at a certain point in time, a unique historical statement of the era's values, condition, and culture. As such, the photographs became important even if they were never published or if no one living could anticipate their eventual use. The growing collection thus became more valuable than any single photograph, regardless of how compelling it might be, because, as Stryker pointed out, one hundred thousand photographs tell a more inclusive story than any single image possibly could.

Therefore, while the Historical Section photographers continued to document both the plight of the rural poor and the efforts of government agencies and programs designed to ameliorate their distress, the photographers began to document as well the growth of a national transportation system and the migration of hundreds of thousands of people from small towns, where they had few hopes, to cities where they dreamed of better prospects. The photographers trained their cameras on the way in which land and people were affected by natural catastrophes, such as the Flood of 1937, the rise of a national tourism, the comforting customs of small-town life, the tremendous variety of the nation's economic life, and the inescapable beauty and vastness of the land. In addition, as the budget of the Historical Section ebbed and flowed according to the government's finances, Stryker struggled to keep photographers on staff by sending them out on assignment for the U.S. Department of Agriculture and loaning them to departments such as Public Health to take photographs of everything from women canning vegetables to children being treated for sore throats. The camera became not just a recording and documenting tool, but a dissecting tool that exposed the nation's social, physical, economic, geographic, and demographic life and laid the parts bare to be analyzed as parts of a larger whole.

By 1941 the Historical Section was a mature organization with an enviable reputation and a seemingly secure future. Its photographs were appearing in all the most widely circulated magazines and newspapers, in books, and in museums. Walker Evans, Dorothea Lange, and Arthur Rothstein were no longer on staff, but Stryker had hired two young photographers, Marion Post, in 1938, and Jack Delano, in 1940, and promoted John Vachon from clerk of the file to photographer. All three were proving to be exceptional, sensitive photographers in the Historical Section mold.

However, the Japanese attack on Pearl Harbor on 7 December 1941 changed the direction and emphasis of their work. Although for at least a year Historical Section photographers had been taking photographs of munitions and plane factories and other examples of war-preparedness, these photographs were extensions of other stories of migrations, work, and values. Now photographic assignments originated deep in the bowels of the bureaucracy, far removed from the goals or interests of either Stryker or the Historical Section photographers. The results were often discouraging. Vachon complained that these forced images of patriotic fervor and effort resembled "those from the Soviet Union."[37]

Even more threatening to the section's future, the Joint Committee on Reduction of Nonessential Federal Expenditures began rooting out what conservative lawmakers deemed government excesses. The Historical Section became one of its targets. Work that had come to be celebrated was now condemned as wasteful in light of the nation's pressing wartime financial needs. Suddenly the kind of sweeping assignments that had put Historical Section photographers on the road for months at a time taking photographs of farms and small towns came to an end.

Supporters in Washington stood up to champion the section and plead for continued funding. Nevertheless, by the early summer of 1942 the Historical Section budget had been cut by a quarter, with plans in 1943 to cut it to almost half its 1941 level. Not surprisingly, Stryker had seen the declaration of war as a photo opportunity, the chance to document the nation as it moved from peacetime to wartime. However, he was unsuccessful in persuading others to adopt his view. Instead, he was forced to lend his photographers to the Office of War Information, and although they continued to find some time on assignments to shoot the kind of photographs they had taken before Pearl Harbor, the OWI soon subsumed the Historical Section. War propaganda overwhelmed the subjects and aesthetics that had made the section famous. Stryker's photographers quickly made career changes. Marion Post, who had recently married widower John Wolcott, had already resigned to rear her new family. Delano and Lee looked for work within the armed services.

Roy Stryker's last major service to the Historical Section was to safeguard the file of 130,000 prints (and approximately 270,000 negatives) for the nation's future. People who had never favored the section's work, as well as those who could see some gain to themselves or their business in possessing some part of the collection, lobbied hard to disperse it. However, desperate to keep the collection intact and accessible, Stryker turned to the Library of Congress, whose director, Archibald MacLeish, was sympathetic to his vision. Jumping over the heads of any number of bureaucrats who wanted some say in the decision, Stryker wrote directly to Jonathan Daniels, administrative assistant to President Roosevelt:

> Preoccupation with the issues of the moment may now lead to the forcible separation of material dealing with today from the material of years before. Such dismemberment would be fatal, for this is a live, an active record. Out of America at peace grew the strength of America at war. This soil is the same soil and the people are the same people.[38]

The gambit succeeded. Reassured that the file would be preserved, Stryker resigned, effective 2 October 1943.

In the almost sixty years since the Historical Section's collection of photographs and negatives was transferred to the Library of Congress, the images have been used countless times to illustrate books and articles about the Great Depression. They have also appeared in hundreds, if not thousands, of exhibitions, including the Museum of Modern Art's 1962 exhibition *The Bitter Years: 1935–1941.* Their continuing availability, which Stryker worked so hard to assure, has made at least a handful of these images a familiar presence in the lives of the American people and icons of the nation's past. However, Stryker never intended that a few photographs would come to represent the complete collection. He always hoped that the file would be considered in its entirety; that a few famous photographs would never obscure the incredible richness of the great body of work from which they had come.

NOTES

1 / Hurley, *Portrait of a Decade,* p. 20.

2 / Stange, "The Record Itself," p. 72.

3 / Hurley, *Portrait of a Decade,* p. 30.

4 / Stryker, job description, 31 May 1934, Library of Congress.

5 / Hurley, *Portrait of a Decade,* p. 36.

6 / *Washington Daily News,* 18 December 1935.

7 / J. Russell Smith was the author or lead co-author of three editions (1925, 1940, 1942) of *North America: Its People and the Resources, Development and Prospects of the Continent as the Home of Man.* M. Odgen Phillips was co-author of the 1940 and 1942 editions.

8 / Stryker interview, p. 26.

9 / Stryker to Rosa Reilly, 22 June 1938. Reilly was an editor at *Popular Photography.*

10 / Lee interview, p. 10

11 / Ibid., p. 9

12 / Mydans, *Carl Mydans,* p. 7.

13 / Mydans interview, p. 13.

14 / Stryker interview, p. 9.

15 / William Morgan to Stryker, 7 July 1938.

16 / Stryker to Grace Falke, 22 April 1937.

17 / Cowles to Stryker, 23 November 1936.

18 / Stryker to Cowles, 13 January 1937.

19 / Stange, "Publicity, Husbandry, and Technology," p. 1.

20 / Stryker to Lange, 23 March 1937.

21 / Stryker to Lange, 17 March 1938.

22 / Historical Section Archive, Library of Congress.

23 / Anderson, p. 143.

24 / Stryker to Post, 21 September 1940.

25 / Hurley, *Portrait of a Decade,* p. 144.

26 / Severin, p. 24.

27 / Stryker to Roosevelt, 24 August 1936.

28 / Stryker to McCamy, 12 April 1938.

29 / Stryker interview, p. 14.

30 / Stryker to Locke, 25 April 1938.

31 / Historical Section Archive, Library of Congress.

32 / Stryker to Arthur Rothstein, 27 May 1938.

33 / Historical Section Archive, Library of Congress.

34 / Hurley, *Marion Post Wolcott,* p. 68.

35 / Rothstein interview, p. 19.

36 / Delano, *Photographic Memories,* p. 85.

37 / Vachon, p. 99.

38 / Hurley, *Portrait of a Decade,* p. 170.

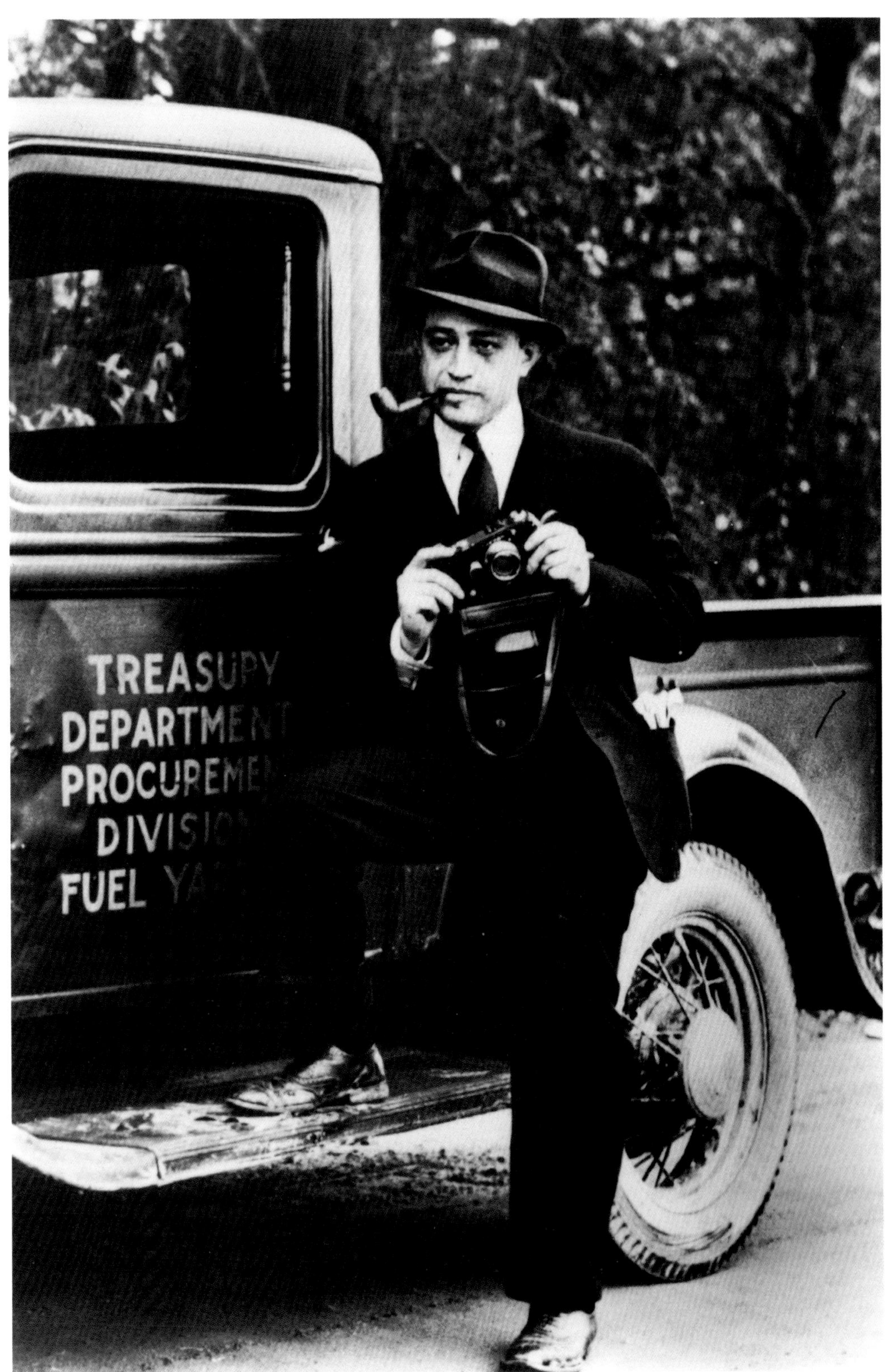

FIGURE 2

Carl Mydans, FSA photographer, full-length portrait, holding camera, with his foot on the running board of a Treasury Department Procurement Division Fuel Yard truck, Washington, D.C., c. 1935.

Carl Mydans

The first Historical Section photographer to receive a major assignment in Vermont was Carl Mydans (fig. 2), who was twenty-nine-years old when he was transferred to the section late in 1935. At the time, the Resettlement Administration was only a year old and the mission that the government had set for the section was clear, even while its director, Roy Stryker, was still determining its field of vision. Mydans brought with him to Vermont not just his camera but also impressions gleaned inevitably both from Stryker's personal experience in the state and from his required reading of Stryker's primary reference, J. Russell Smith's *North America*. According to Smith, the Vermont that Mydans encountered was a hardscrabble place forged by a difficult climate, generations of hard labor in the woods and fields, and a challenging landscape.

Mydans likely took advantage of Stryker's cottage on eighty wooded acres on Lake Eden. Stryker built the cottage on land he had purchased in 1931 for $1,000, and he used the retreat regularly for summer vacations with his wife, Alice.[1] It must have suited Mydans's criteria. In all his travels for the Historical Section he chose his overnight resting places carefully because he insisted on developing his film every night before he went to bed. For this he needed ice-cold running water.[2] While on assignment in Vermont, Mydans's travels were restricted to a giant, lopsided horseshoe that ran from Newport down Route 100 to Hyde Park, then over Route 15 to Hardwick and up Route 14 to Irasburg. Stryker's cottage lay directly along the southwest prong of the route and would have afforded free lodging to someone whose employer was always strapped for funding. As a starting point for photographing Vermont, this foray offered interesting possibilities, particularly the chance to witness some of the more isolated and depressed aspects of Vermont.

In 1936 Mydans, who had graduated from Boston University's School of Journalism in 1930, was already an established journalist whose byline had appeared in the *Boston Globe* and the *Boston Herald*. He thought of himself as a print journalist who occasionally took photographs. He worked with a Graflex, an awkward box camera with a mirror, but after he moved to New York City in 1931 to become a staff writer for the *American Banker* he took photography courses at the Brooklyn Institute of Arts and Sciences and purchased one of only two kinds of 35mm cameras then on the market[3]: a 35mm Zeiss Contax, which the majority of serious photographers then regarded as a toy because it could produce images that were grainy or fuzzy.[4] He began freelancing, and sold most of his early work to *Time* magazine, whose editor, Daniel Lonwell, eventually passed his name along to Robert Thorpe at the Resettlement Administration. Thorpe recruited him to work for the Department of Interior.[5] The two men collaborated briefly on a book about suburban resettlement that was never published, but near the end of 1935 Mydans was transferred within the RA to the Historical Section. He was the first, but not the last, photographer to come to the section with a background in photojournalism. Perhaps more significantly, he was one of the first professional photographers in the country to be enthusiastic about shooting with a 35mm camera.[6]

From the moment that Mydans began taking photographs with his Contax, he believed in the possibilities of the 35mm format. Small, lightweight, and easily portable, Mydans's camera gave him flexibility and speed not afforded by larger cameras, particularly in capturing people's spontaneous expressions. He liked that he could wear it, not just carry it around; that he could manipulate it as an extension of his eyes rather than as a bulky piece of equipment at the end of his arm.[7]

Mydans's first assignment, in March 1936, was to visit the deep South and "to do cotton."[8] The assignment was a shock for a number of reasons, not the least of which was the young journalist's ignorance of the South's culture and economy. As Mydans was leaving the office to embark on this inaugural assignment, Stryker asked him what he knew about cotton. Mydans's reply, "Not much," caused Stryker to delay the photographer's departure while he introduced his new employee to the kind of discussions about subjects and regions that would later become almost routine in the section's office. Freshly educated, Mydans spent almost five months in the South, where the poverty and working conditions touched him deeply.

Later that same summer Mydans made his second and final trip for the government. He drove north from Washington, first through Vermont and then through New Hampshire. Before the trip ended, he had spent a total of four months on the road, and the range of photographs he shot reveals how quickly the Historical Section's focus on the rural poor was expanding to encompass other themes

Charged specifically with capturing scenes that would convey Vermont's rural poverty, Mydans struck a delicate balance, trying not to portray isolation, backwardness, or desperate economic conditions as quaint. An abandoned factory and an abandoned farm, both in Newport, and a series on cutover and burned-over land in Troy all convey loss unequivocally. The farm scene especially, with a wrecked car and a yard strewn with artifacts belonging to some previous owner, is a stark image of failed lives (fig. 3). A farmer tending sheep in the vicinity of North Troy in a field cobbled with stones, a woman in a long skirt waiting in a buggy outside the general store in Lowell, a dilapidated privy attached precariously to an old farmhouse, and a short series of photographs taken at an auction in Hyde Park are more subtle images of a land impoverished by annual harvests of rocks and a people frustrated by efforts to keep pace with economic developments elsewhere in the nation.

However, Mydans also directed his camera to subjects beyond that of Vermont's poverty. In August and September he attended fairs in Morrisville and Albany, respectively. He was fascinated by the people attending them, particularly elderly fairgoers, many of whom he photographed candidly in their Sunday dresses and suits. He was also interested in the range of activity at the fairs: farm families, who clearly regarded the local fair as their annual vacation, setting up camp and stringing their laundry from the hoods of their Model Ts to nearby fenceposts (fig. 4); horse and cattle judging; parades and bands; sideshow booths and grandstand events. Mydans's fair photographs are striking because of the seriousness with which this summer treat is being enjoyed. Capturing wonderfully, perhaps in caricature, the Yankee penchant for dourness, Mydans's photographs of fairgoers with unsmiling faces rely on the spatial relationships among his subjects to convey both a strong sense of individualism and an equally strong sense of community.

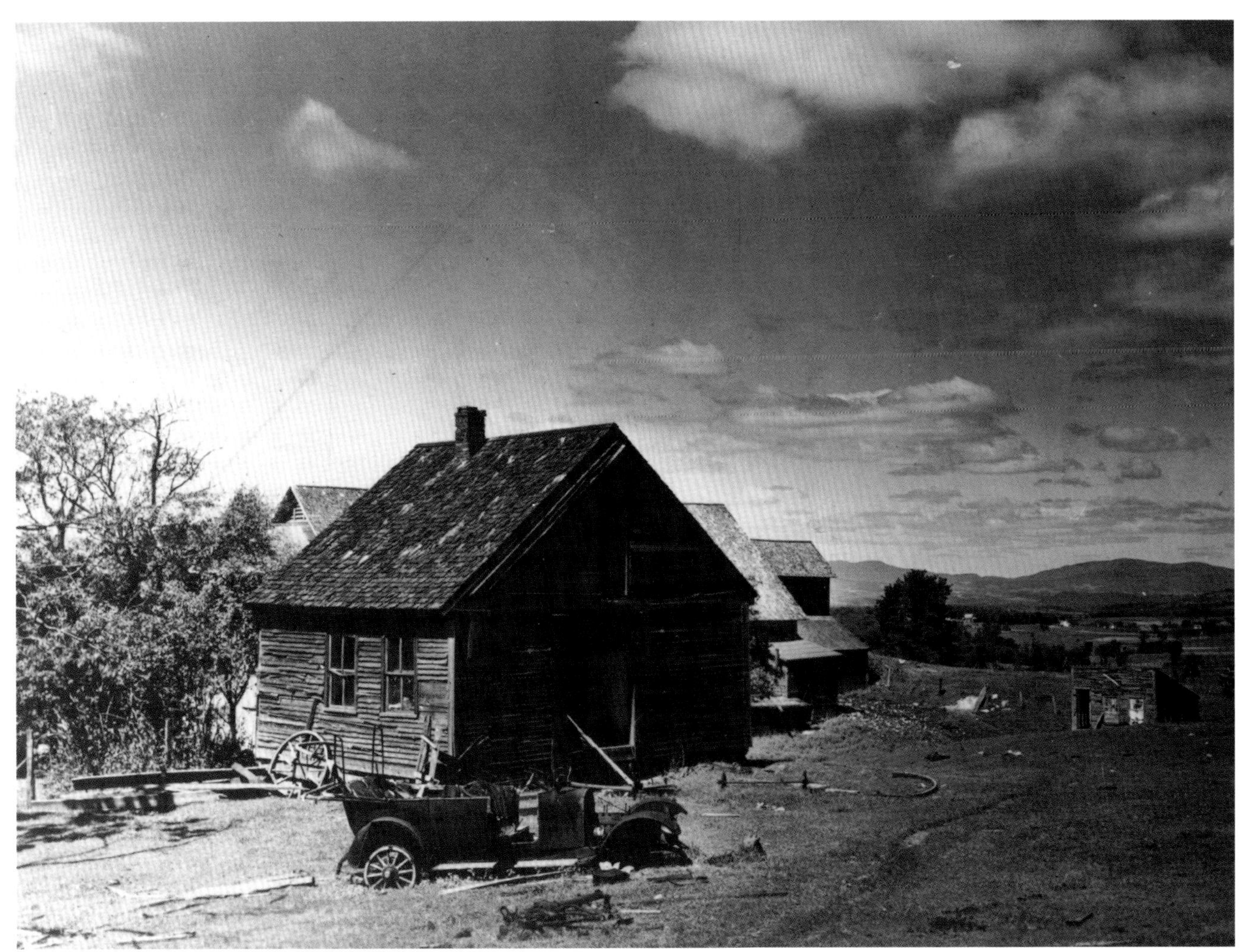

FIGURE 3
Carl Mydans
Newport (vicinity), Vt.
August 1936. Old abandoned farmhouse.

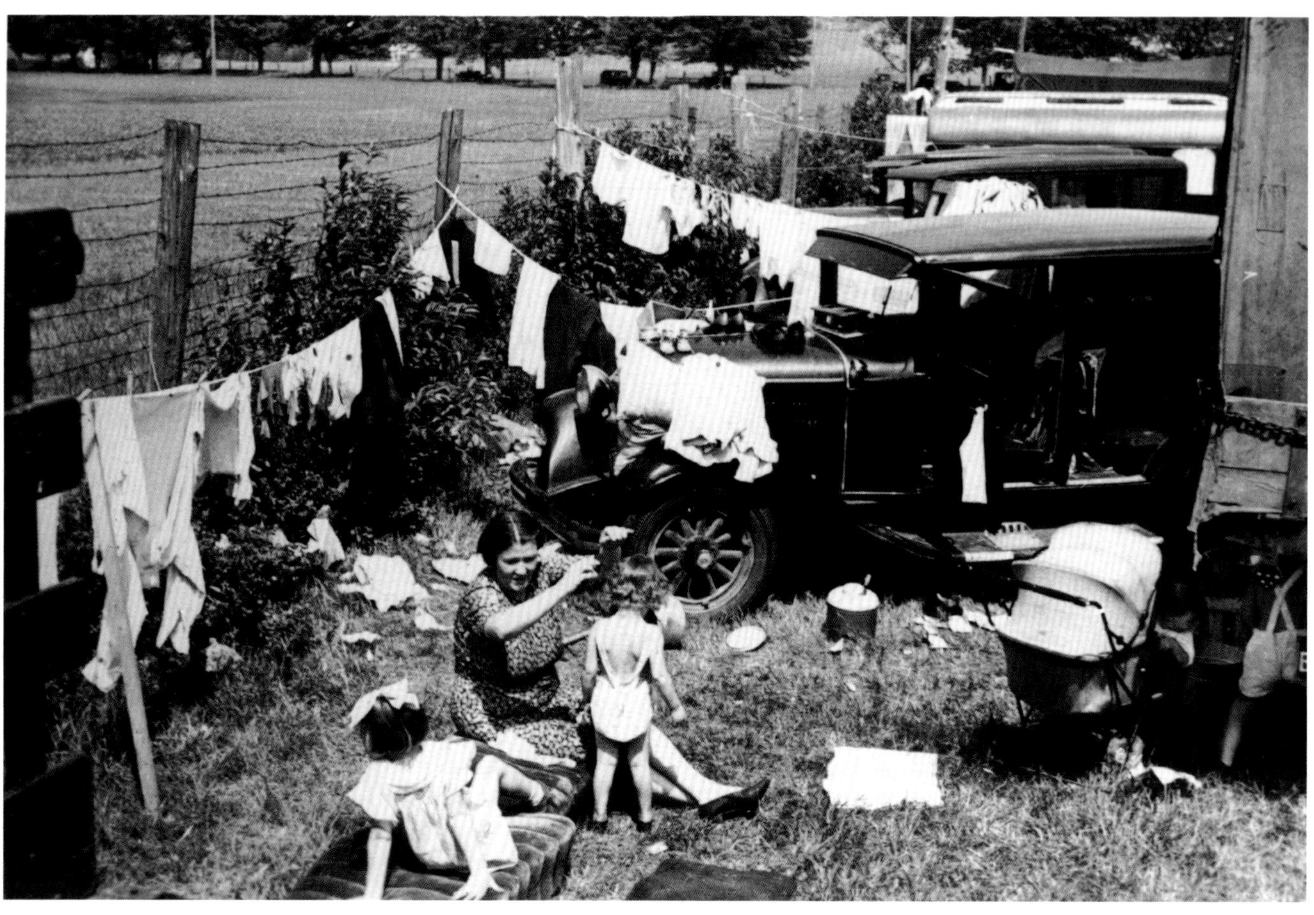

FIGURE 4
Carl Mydans
Morrisville, Vt. August. 1936. Farm families come prepared to live at the annual fair.

One Vermont photograph by Mydans deserves specific mention. Although Historical Section photographers were criticized repeatedly for being tools of FDR's New Deal, this charge was leveled with particular vehemence during the autumn of 1936. The vocal accusers were mainly Republicans who felt that the presidential election was being manipulated by government photographs overdramatizing the nation's plight and unduly crediting Democratic solutions. Mydans, speaking decades later, was one of those who believed the Historical Section's photographs did influence the election's outcome. Perhaps he was trying to show rural support for Roosevelt when he photographed a rare sight during his swing through Vermont in the fall of 1936. This scene in downtown Hardwick (fig. 5) is surprising because a large Roosevelt banner is strung across the street, suggesting enthusiastic local support of the Democratic president in what was at that time a traditionally conservative and Republican state. (No doubt the presence of local granite quarries had created a pocket of pro-labor Democrats, but the sentiment was not widely shared in Vermont. When the votes were counted in November only Vermont and Maine failed to join the majority of Americans in supporting the incumbent president.) Just as surprising is a second large banner strung across the main street, this one urging voters with a social conscience to support the enactment of the radical employment and economic relief initiative known as the Townsend Plan, even though the passage of the Social Security Act a year earlier virtually precluded that. Finally, a small banner in the background promotes Alf Landon, FDR's Republican opponent.

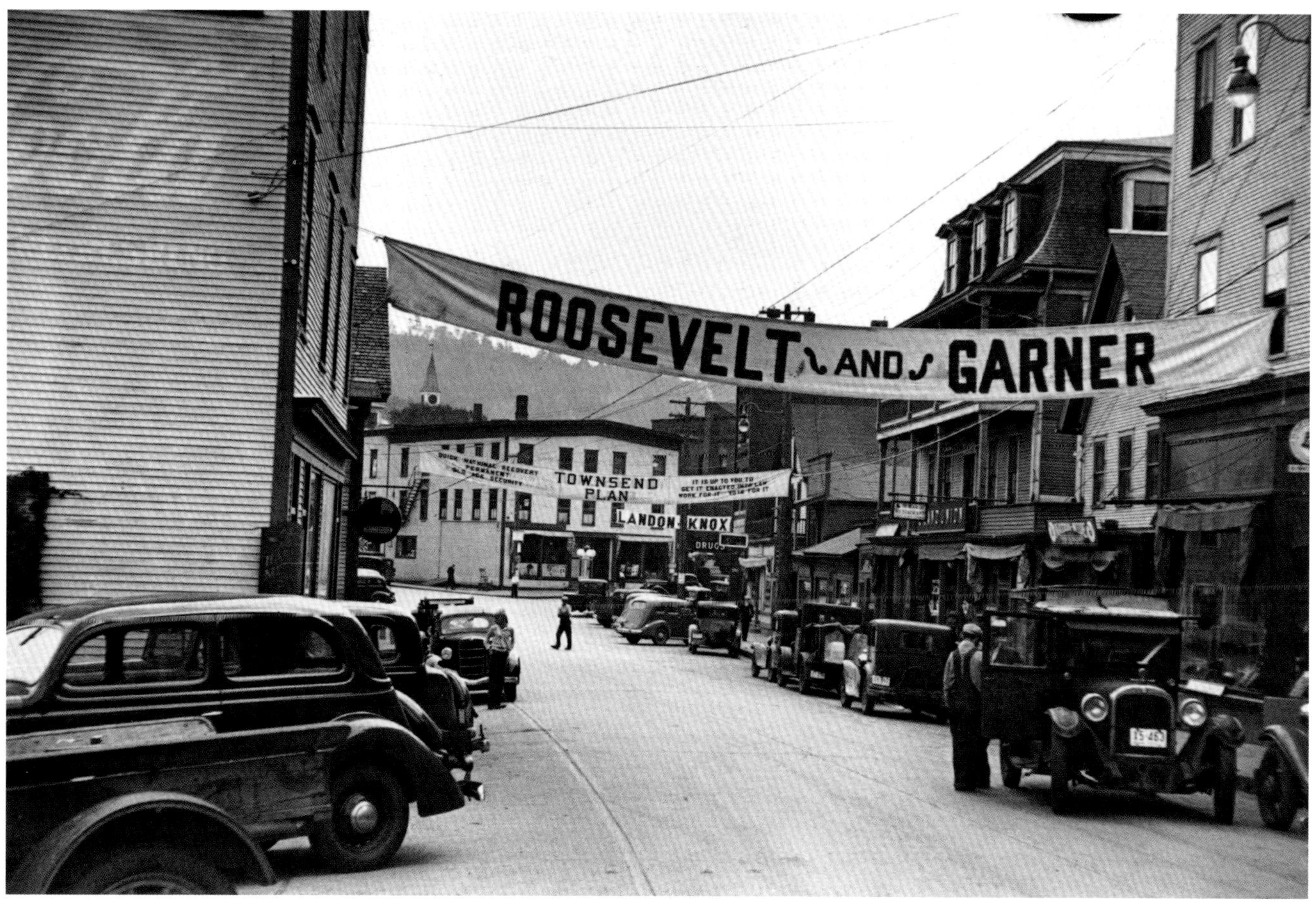

FIGURE 5
Carl Mydans
Hardwick, Vt. September 1936. Political banner.

Two other sets of Mydans's Historical Section photographs in Vermont are noteworthy. One is a breathtaking series of landscapes in which small farms, tended fields, and gentle hills are dwarfed by huge, cloud-filled skies. The sense that humans and their endeavors are simply a small part of a vast, impersonal universe is dramatic and inescapable. The second set is of a farmer's dairy cooperative in Hardwick. From time to time over the next six years, Historical Section photographers in Vermont would photograph farmer's cooperatives, perhaps hoping to portray them as a powerful force in restoring economic parity and dignity to rural life.

Finally, Mydans shot several photographs of Forrest Carpenter, a hired hand and sometime delinquent taxpayer in Eden Mills. Mydans was no doubt drawn to Carpenter by the subject's photogenic face, but Carpenter would become one of the few Vermonters to appear in the work of successive photographers who also based themselves at Stryker's Lake Eden cottage. Mydans's images of Carpenter are noteworthy for another reason, as well. They were the first of hundreds of portraits of Vermonters that made their way into the Historical Section file between 1936 and 1942. The photographers were not driven solely by the aesthetics of particular faces. Rather, according to Mydans, Stryker believed the nation's collective pain during the later years of the depression was etched on individual faces. In his book *Carl Mydans: Photojournalist*, Mydans recalls being sent out on his early Historical Section assignments with an admonition from his director:

> "You will see this is a period of disaster in the United States . . . and I think you are going to find what is happening in the faces of the people." . . . I did, and what I mostly photographed in those months of travel in America was people and their faces.[9]

The result in Vermont of Stryker's insight and directive was the start of a large, invaluable album of portraits reflecting every emotion from despair to joy, from grimness to indomitability.

Mydans left the Historical Section shortly after he returned from his New England swing, lured away by *Life* magazine while the first issue was going to press in the autumn of 1936.[10] Reflecting decades later on his experience with the Historical Section, Mydans said that he had gained more from it than he had given. He admitted that one of the most indelible lessons he had gleaned from his work there had less to do with photography than with sociology—with, indeed, Stryker's driving vision:

> I think the most exciting thing to me was to learn about America and perhaps of all the things I saw I was most impressed by the people. They differed in the various parts of the country on one hand, but on the other, they were very much alike. I became distinctly aware of how American all Americans are.[11]

In addition, Mydans credited Stryker with teaching him important aesthetic lessons, particularly about standards of technical and artistic excellence and how to recognize when a photograph is "right." He interpreted this as a photograph's capacity to tell a story.[12] He learned his lessons well, and throughout his long career with *Life*, *Time*, and *Smithsonian* magazines, he distinguished himself as a modern photojournalist.

NOTES

1 / Land deed, Eden Town Clerk's office, Eden, Vermont, 19 February 1931.

2 / Mydans, *Carl Mydans*, p. 19.

3 / Ibid., p. 17.

4 / Ibid., p. 16.

5 / Ibid.

6 / O'Neal, p. 115.

7 / Mydans interview, p. 13.

8 / O'Neal, p. 115.

9 / Ibid., p. 19

10 / Mydans, *Carl Mydans*, p. 16.

11 / O'Neal, p. 116.

12 / Mydans, *Carl Mydans*, pp. 16, 18.

Arthur Rothstein

When Arthur Rothstein ventured into Windsor County, Vermont, in February 1936, he became the first Historical Section photographer to visit the state (fig. 6). The sojourn was part of a longer swing through New England, but his stay in the state was so brief, the results for the fledgling file so negligible, that it is hard to learn much of anything from this inaugural trip to Vermont. Although approximately a dozen images of the state survive in the file mislabeled "Windsor County, New Hampshire," only two shots of the farmers' cooperative in White River Junction are correctly identified as Vermont images.

According to an article in the *Washington Post*, Arthur Rothstein was a "serious young man [who] looks much older than his 24 years. He is rather short with the build of a hard-punching middleweight. He speaks in a serious, concise manner and he seems to whip out his words in a firm, convincing voice."[1] Although Rothstein became a tireless road photographer for the Historical Section, nothing in that description suggests he possessed the kind of stoic fatalism that has always served residents of the North Country well in coping with their environment, especially in winter. Indeed, looking back at his first New England visit, he said it was technically the hardest work he ever did for the Historical Section. He reserved a special complaint for how difficult it was to work with frozen equipment.[2]

Arthur Rothstein next ventured into Vermont in May 1937, nine months after Mydans's visit. As soon as he crossed the border into the state, he became the only photographer to visit Vermont more than once on behalf of the Historical Section. This time Rothstein came as a government photographer on loan from the Historical Section of the Resettlement Administration to the Agricultural Assistance Administration. Renting out his photographers was one way Stryker raised enough money to keep the section's work afloat. However, the trip was unsuccessful for a variety of reasons, not the least because the AAA later balked at paying its bill. Only a handful of photographs that Rothstein took during the tour—photographs taken in Johnson and Woodstock—eventually made their way into the Historical Section file, but on the other hand, most of the photographs were never intended for the file. According to a letter to Stryker dated 12 June 1937 from H. W. Soule, executive officer of the Vermont Agricultural Conservation Program, Rothstein was accompanied on his May tour of Vermont by a program representative who wrote a "legend" for the photographs so the entire package could be converted into a government filmstrip. In the letter, Soule expresses hope that Rothstein will be able to return to Vermont "to get pictures showing the results of some of the practices," but there is no evidence this happened.[3] Among the Rothstein photographs that survive from this assignment, one reflects most clearly the work that he would have been documenting for the AAA in Vermont. It is a poignant, anonymous portrait of an RA client, one Vermonter among untold others who

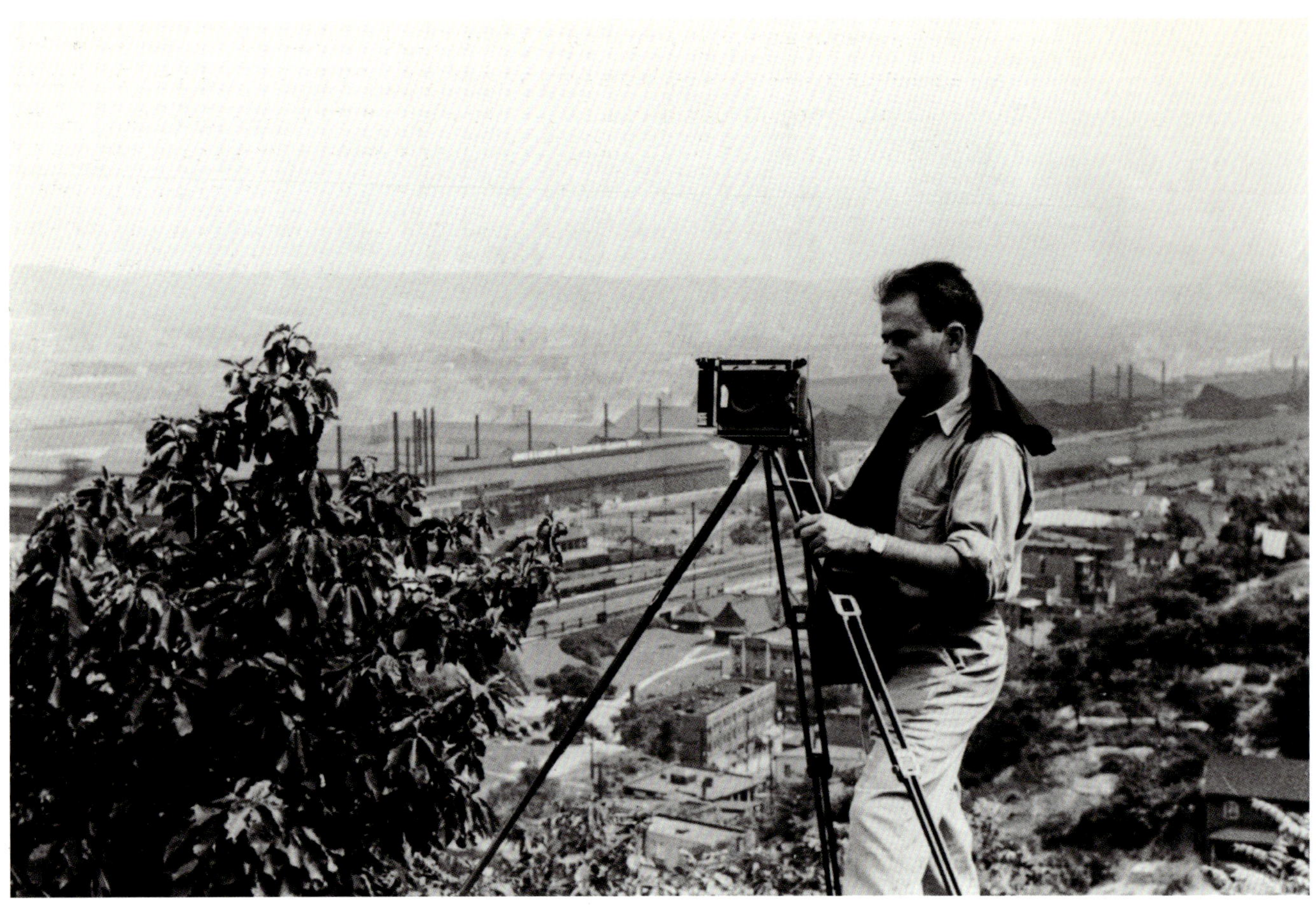

FIGURE 6
Arthur Rothstein, FSA photographer, 1938.

were transplanted from unproductive farms to either more productive ones or employment in one of the state's cities or larger towns.

Of all the Historical Section photographers, Rothstein may have been most patient about working in severely restricted circumstances, such as those imposed by the AAA, because his first work at the section was similarly tightly controlled. Only twenty-two in 1937, he had met Stryker several years earlier while a sophomore at Columbia University. He was taking the laboratory course in economics and government that Stryker taught by dragging his students all over New York City to witness the practical exercise of both in the workplace, in stores, in labor and union halls, and in city hall. Rothstein, who founded the Columbia Camera Club as an undergraduate, was a whiz at camera technology and already an award-winning photographer when he met Stryker. While Rothstein was still an undergraduate, Stryker hired him as part of the National Youth Project to reproduce photographs for a book on American agriculture that he was compiling, and the young photographer honed his skills doing this technically demanding but uninspiring copy work until the project fell apart.[4] By then, Stryker had accepted a job with the RA, and he approached his young protégé about coming to Washington to help set up the Historical Section. Rothstein, whose dreams of going to medical school or doing graduate work in chemistry had been dashed by the depression, packed his camera and moved from his native New York City to Washington a month after earning his diploma, becoming the first photographer that Stryker hired.[5]

At first the photography work was as dry as the copy work that preceded it. Rothstein's assignment was to set up a darkroom and to photograph every piece of paper directed to the office as a way of establishing an archive of the RA's work, but as Stryker's vision of the work of the Historical Section expanded, Rothstein was able to branch out into more satisfying work. His first big road assignment was to travel through the Shenandoah Valley, where the federal government was buying up land to create a national park, and to document the lives of the people who were being displaced by the plan.[6] Like Mydans—but unlike most other professional photographers of the time—he enjoyed working with a 35mm camera, whose small size helped him develop a technique he called "the unobtrusive camera." Years later he described that technique as "the idea of becoming part of the environment that people are in to such an extent that they're not even aware that pictures are being taken."[7]

Stryker was also fond of the possibilities miniature cameras offered and aware that Mydans and Rothstein were setting precedent by experimenting with them. In an undated document entitled "The Miniature Camera in Resettlement Administration Photography," Stryker claimed that "Excellent miniature equipment plus imaginative technicians [in the Historical Section] have combined to set a new mark in governmental photography." He pointed out that when the Historical Section's photographers were photographing people, miniature cameras were used "almost exclusively because of the ease of handling and the unobtrusiveness peculiar to this instrument. Nothing is posed—people are caught unaware in that instant which reveals their essential qualities to the photographer."[8]

Thrilled with the images Rothstein brought back from the Shenandoah Valley, Stryker sent him on his brief foray into New England in the winter of 1936, and then in spring of the same year dispatched him to the Midwest, where, amid the desiccated landscape and swirling dust, he ruined his Zeiss Super Ikonta B camera, permanently damaged his right eye, and shot *Dust Storm, Cimarron County, 1936*, which made him famous.[9] The image—a father and his two young sons, their heads bowed before a driving dust storm—impressed upon the nation, as no single photograph had before, the desperate plight of the land in the Midwest and the people who worked it. Like Dorothea Lange's *Migrant Mother, Dust Storm, Cimarron County, 1936* became one of the handful of images for which the section would be forever known.

On this trip Rothstein also took the infamous photographs of the bleached steer skull that branded the Historical Section's photographs unfavorably for months to come. When the story broke in August 1936, and newspapers across the country began questioning the integrity of the section's work, Stryker's new assistant, Edwin Locke, had to act as the agency spokesman because Stryker was away from Washington, relaxing at his cottage on Lake Eden in Vermont. Although he quickly hopped a train back to the capital, Stryker was too far from the eye of the storm to direct immediate damage control during one of the biggest crises ever to hit the section.[10]

By the time Rothstein returned East to New England a year later, he had completed a long swing through the South and one through the West, traveling as far as Washington state. He arrived in Vermont at the end of August 1937. His companion on this, his third trip to the state, was Roy Stryker, who wrote to Grace Falke, Rexford Tugwell's assistant, that he had been hoping for weeks to get away to Vermont as soon as he could to vacation at his cottage on Lake Eden.[11] If Stryker's letters can be believed, his visit to Vermont was supposed to be restful; however, it is doubtful that a man of his nervous temperament was ever truly at rest. Indeed, Stryker often used his vacations in Vermont to recharge his energy and plot his agency's future. Writing to another Historical Section photographer near the end of September, having just returned from Vermont to Washington, Stryker claimed "I feel like a new person; had a grand vacation; got lots of things done; met and talked to lots of people; hatched a whole new set of ideas on documentary photography."[12]

A map of Rothstein's travels suggests that he, like Mydans, made the Stryker cottage a base for at least some of his work. He retraced Mydans's horseshoe from Newport to Irasburg, which took him neatly past the Stryker cottage, but he also branched out considerably, the most obvious line following Route 108 from Jeffersonville south to Stowe, and then Route 100 south from Stowe to Stockbridge. Along the way he made detours to Burlington and Winooski, Plainfield, and Bethel. Stops in Northfield, Bethel, and Woodstock suggest that he followed Route 12, and shots from Brattleboro suggest that he either entered or left the state through its southeast corner. One set of photographs taken in Kirby, a small village on a still-unpaved road between East Lyndon and Concord, shows that he spent time in the Northeast Kingdom, Vermont's remote northeastern-most counties. Apparently, Stryker accompanied Rothstein during at least some of the travel. Writing to Dorothea Lange in California at the end of September, Stryker acknowledged,

> I am finally back from a rather long stay in the north country. I managed to get some pretty good rest out of my stay, and also accomplished some interesting research. Arthur and I got a lot of interesting pictures.[13]

FIGURE 7
Arthur Rothstein
Windsor County, Vt. September 1937. Cutting hay.

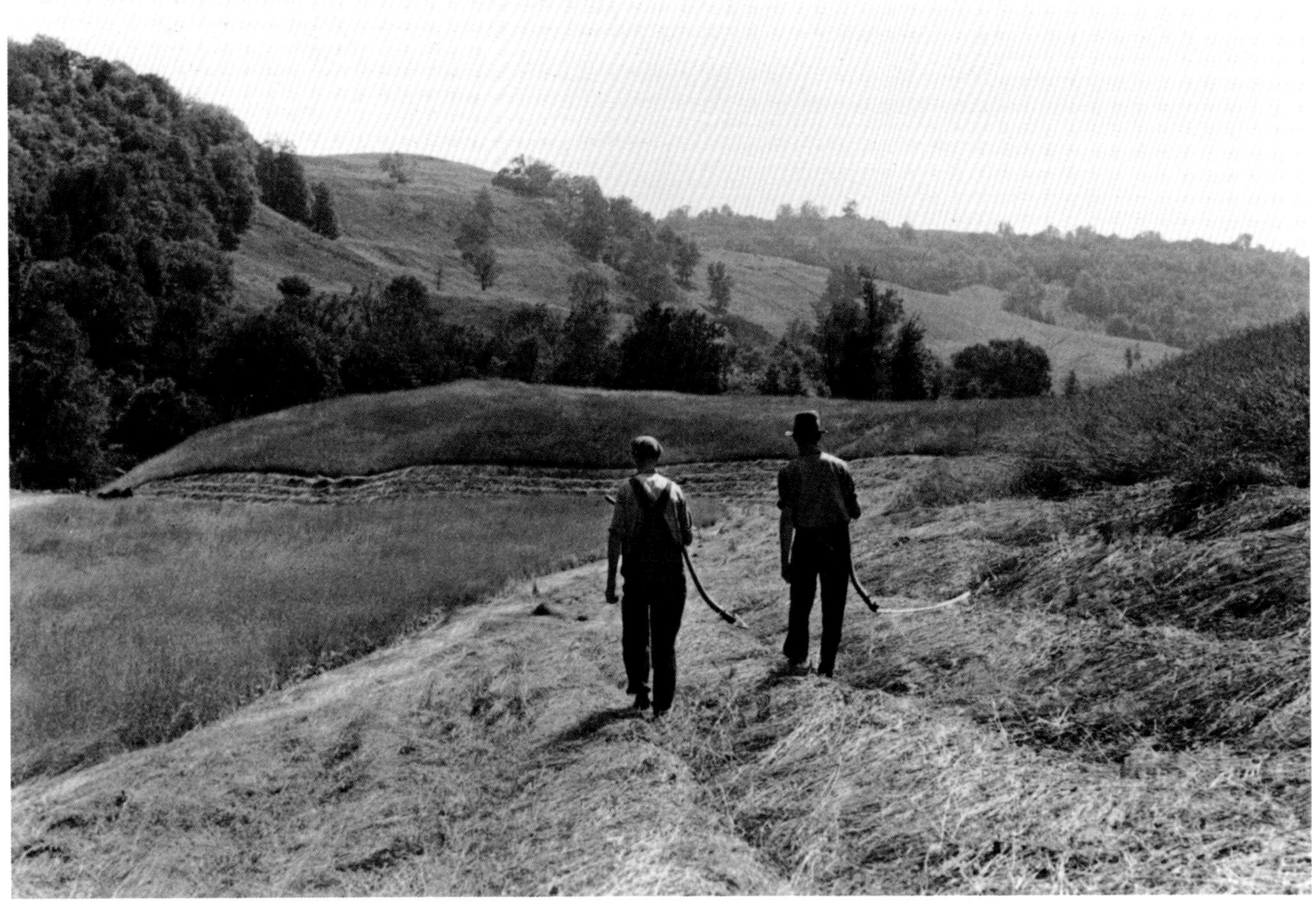

Rothstein's photographs of Vermont in 1937, taken when his boss could directly influence his choice of subject, are evidence that the field of Stryker's vision was expanding as he interpreted the scope of the section's work more and more inclusively. Rothstein's photographs also reflect a distinctly different sensibility at work behind the viewfinder than Mydans's work had demonstrated. Pictures of cutover land in Chittenden County and Irasburg, and pictures of eroded land and an abandoned farm in Caledonia County echo the themes of Mydans's photographs a year earlier. However, in other aspects, their landscapes are quite different. Where Mydans captured farms from great distances, conveying a sense of loss and vulnerability by their diminished size under a glowering sky, Rothstein worked closer up. The skies are still dramatic—Rothstein sometimes used a filter, which few other Historical Section photographers did—but the farms are populated by people hard at work threshing, haying, scything, and generally applying themselves to their land and their future (fig. 7).[14] However dirty the work (and the threshing photographs exude sweat and grime), these are images of human commitment, as compelling as any of silos and ripened fields in projecting the idea that as long as people are willing to work, all is not lost.

In fact, the theme of human labor pervades Rothstein's images. It seems both redemptive and instructive, as if he is spreading Stryker's gospel that work and the indomitable human spirit will sustain the nation through the depression regardless of how dark the prospects look. Branching out beyond the farm, Rothstein photographed blacksmiths, lumber-mill workers, railroad workers (fig. 8), veneer-mill workers, woodcutters, kitchenware painters, and storekeepers. When the workers themselves were not available, he captured the spirit of labor in a sign, "Workers of the World Unite at the Ballot Box," painted on a barn door in Rochester. The unmistakable message conveyed by Rothstein's photographs is that Vermonters are facing the depression by refusing to lie down and die.

In his streetscapes, Rothstein also did not dwell on the grim. His photographs of downtown Randolph, Stowe, Morrisville, and several other Vermont communities show streets often curiously empty of people but clearly possessing the character of established and durable places. In their own way—by showing complex webs of power and telephone lines, mileage signs to distant places, and the intersections of paved roads that clearly sustain the state's commerce—Rothstein's images also further Stryker's interest in showing the nation's enterprise and interconnectedness.

Process was, in fact, quickly becoming one of the Historical Section's themes. Stryker was fascinated by relationships, by how things happened, and by what the connections were among them. This explains, in part, the unusual set of photographs Rothstein took of the McNally farm in Kirby, approximately two dozen of which made it into the file. Within this sequence of photographs of a small Guernsey dairy farm, Rothstein documented the scope and intensity of the work needed to make the farm successful, and also turned his lens on the division of labor among the McNallys and their hired help. Small farms such as this, isolated by geography and slow to follow the trend in the dairy industry from lower-producing Jerseys and Guernseys to higher-producing Holsteins, were thorns in the side of the FSA, which sought to shift farmers to more productive land and more efficient operations. However, Rothstein's series clearly melds images of technological progress, such as milking machines and bottling equipment, with those of character traits such as industriousness and determination.

Like Mydans a year earlier, Rothstein also turned his camera on Stryker's neighbors in

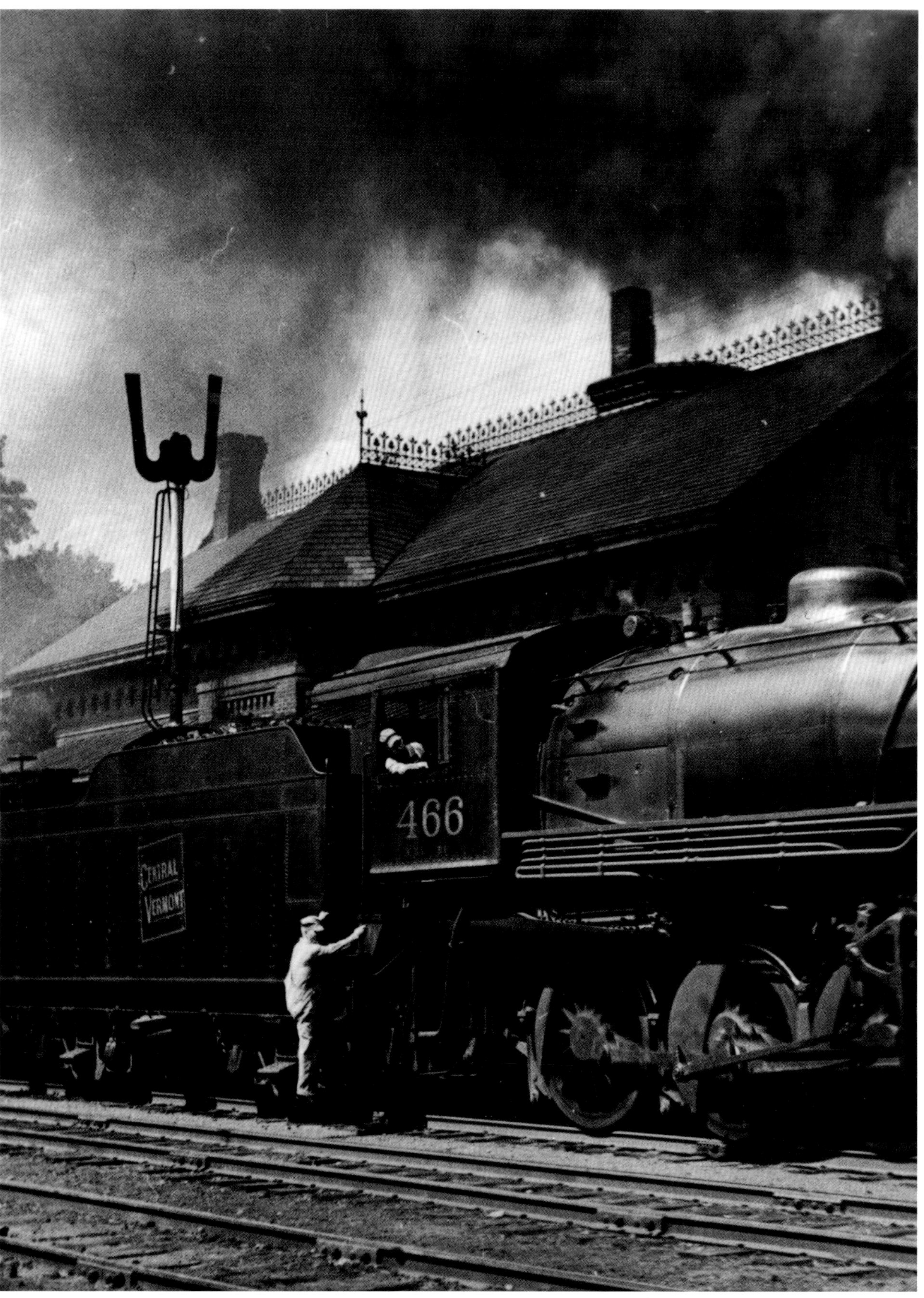
466
CENTRAL VERMONT

FIGURE 8 (opposite)
Arthur Rothstein
Randolph, Vt. September 1937. Scene at the railroad station.

Eden Mills. More than thirty photographs of residents of the town of Eden were selected for the file, including three more portraits of hired hand Forrest Carpenter. Carpenter was an interesting subject for repeated study. Cited frequently in Eden town reports throughout these years as a delinquent taxpayer, he was neither a farmer nor a tenant farmer (therefore, not likely to be an RA or FSA client), but his marginal existence certainly represented the bleak depths of the depression. It is also possible that he was merely close at hand, that he was caretaker of the Stryker cottage when the Strykers were not in residence, or that he simply possessed an interesting face.

Rothstein also captured a broader view of the town, and in these portraits he demonstrated a technique that Walker Evans brought to the Historical Section in its earliest days and one that Stryker encouraged. "Roy [Stryker] was the one who made me aware of the fact that there is a great deal of significance in small details," Rothstein said in an interview years later. "He made me aware of the fact that it was important, say, to photograph the corner of a cabin showing an old shoe and a bag of flour; or it was important to get a close-up of a man's face; and it was important to show a window stuffed with rags."[15] Rothstein included exactly these kinds of visual clues in portraits that give his subjects dramatic context. He photographed the Eden town clerk, for example, standing beside the town safe, and Perley Mosley, a trapper, holding three luxuriant fox pelts. Rothstein also spent time on Frank Kinney's farm in Eden Mills. Unlike his photographs of the McNally farm, those of the Kinney farm are mostly family portraits that show little of the actual work that sustains a farm, but they do capture members of the family and hired help in the context of place: sitting atop a hayrack, preparing meals and talking in the kitchen, posing behind a window in their home, sawing pulpwood.

Rothstein also stopped by at least three fairs, a small one in Craftsbury in early September, the large state fair in Rutland, and the Champlain Exposition in Essex Junction. At the two large fairs, in particular, he was able to practice his "unobtrusive-camera" technique using a small 35mm camera. Just as Mydans arranged his landscapes to convey an impression of man's insignificance, and his fair photographs to portray the stereotypically severe New England Yankee, Rothstein applied a lighter hand to landscapes and looked for similarly lighter subject material for his fair photographs. At the Rutland fair, he found his subjects on the midway, where he photographed fairgoers enjoying the barking at side shows advertising nudes and swing dancers, among other attractions, and he captured the crowd's pleasure and interest in the diversion provided by their surroundings.

In the only instance of two employees of the Historical Section taking photographs in Vermont at the same time, Edwin Locke was also working his way around Central Vermont while Rothstein was photographing the state's fairs. Locke, Assistant Chief of the Historical Section from 1935 to 1937, was not an official photographer for the section; rather, he spent most of his time dealing with administrative matters. However, occasionally the temptation to pick up a camera himself must have been overwhelming. He was in Vermont in August and September of 1937, as part of a fast-paced, ten-state swing that took him from Maryland north to New England. Roughly a dozen of the photographs he took during this visit to the state made their way into the file.[16] All of them are from the same region—from Proctor on the west to White River Junction on the east. One is captioned *A Marble Storeyard. Ripley, Vermont. August 1937*, but there is no such place. The wonder is that more labeling mistakes were not made, considering that photographers were often miles farther along on their travels before they sat down to caption the prints that Stryker's darkroom

FIGURE 9 (opposite)
Arthur Rothstein
Kirby, Vt. September 1937. Looking for the mail on the McNally farm.

team in Washington had developed and returned to them. In this case, in light of Locke's concentrated work in one area of the state, the caption should probably read, *Ripley and Sons Marble Works, Center Rutland, Vermont. August 1937.* Locke's contribution was small, but it was an interesting addition to the section's collage portrait of Vermont, showing at one extreme relatively rare photographs of a Vermont covered bridge and an old tombstone, and at the other, a modern service station and the ingenuity of a family living near Woodstock who had mounted their mailbox on a pulley.

Two months after returning to Washington, Arthur Rothstein took a two-week leave to work at *Look*, which had been launched the previous spring. Stryker was disappointed but not surprised. He wrote to another Historical Section photographer that Rothstein has been "restless since Carl [Mydans] got his job at *Life*. He has by spells done excellent work, but underneath it all he has been decidedly restless."[17] Like Mydans, Rothstein was looking for stability. The Historical Section never offered that to any of its photographers. As budgets went up and down, photographers, especially the temperamental Dorothea Lange, were let go and rehired. Rothstein soon returned to the section, ultimately covering more territory than did any other section photographer, but he stayed only until the early spring of 1940. Soon after, Rothstein was once again lured to *Look* by the possibility of being named a staff photographer. Perhaps then he felt he had gone as far as he could with the Historical Section. Perhaps, too, he could see war on the horizon and understood instinctively that the nature of his government work would soon change dramatically. On 6 April 1940, two days after Rothstein had submitted his letter of resignation, Stryker wrote to Vernon Pope, editor of *Look*, conceding that "I hate like hell to lose the boy, but you take him with my blessing. . . . Of course, losing Arthur is more than just losing a photographer: he came with me when this place started, and of course, there are ties other than those through the photographer and the camera."[18]

Although one of Rothstein's peers once wrote that he was famous for "photographing the wretched of the earth," Rothstein's work in Vermont does not reflect this.[19] His images of farmers scything are reminiscent of nineteenth-century Barbizon paintings of peasants working golden fields of grain, their postures and frozen movements implying a liquid grace born of long practice. His photographs of crowds milling around outlandish sideshows at the state fair are irresistibly amusing. If there is a hard, realistic edge in Rothstein's photographs of the McNallys at work, there is also a gentler quality and an implicit message that this family is linked to the outside world; for example, in the photograph of the McNally son checking the mailbox (fig. 9). Except in the grim pictures of the chaff-covered threshers, Rothstein portrays a state that is holding its own against the depression.

Indeed, Rothstein's images, like all the others in the file, convey a more complex message than they suggest at first glance. On the one hand, they document the era's undeniable need, both human and environmental. On the other hand, they often portray, particularly in some of the more self-conscious portraits, irresistible human qualities such as resilience and fortitude that border on defiance. These themes grew tangled in New Deal politics. For the Democrats, the photographs justified their work and the government's ever-expanding menu of programs. Many Republicans, in contrast, pointed to the images of self-reliance as proof that Americans were capable of facing the crisis brought on by the depression without radical government intervention. In short, both parties were capable of using the photographs to their own ends.

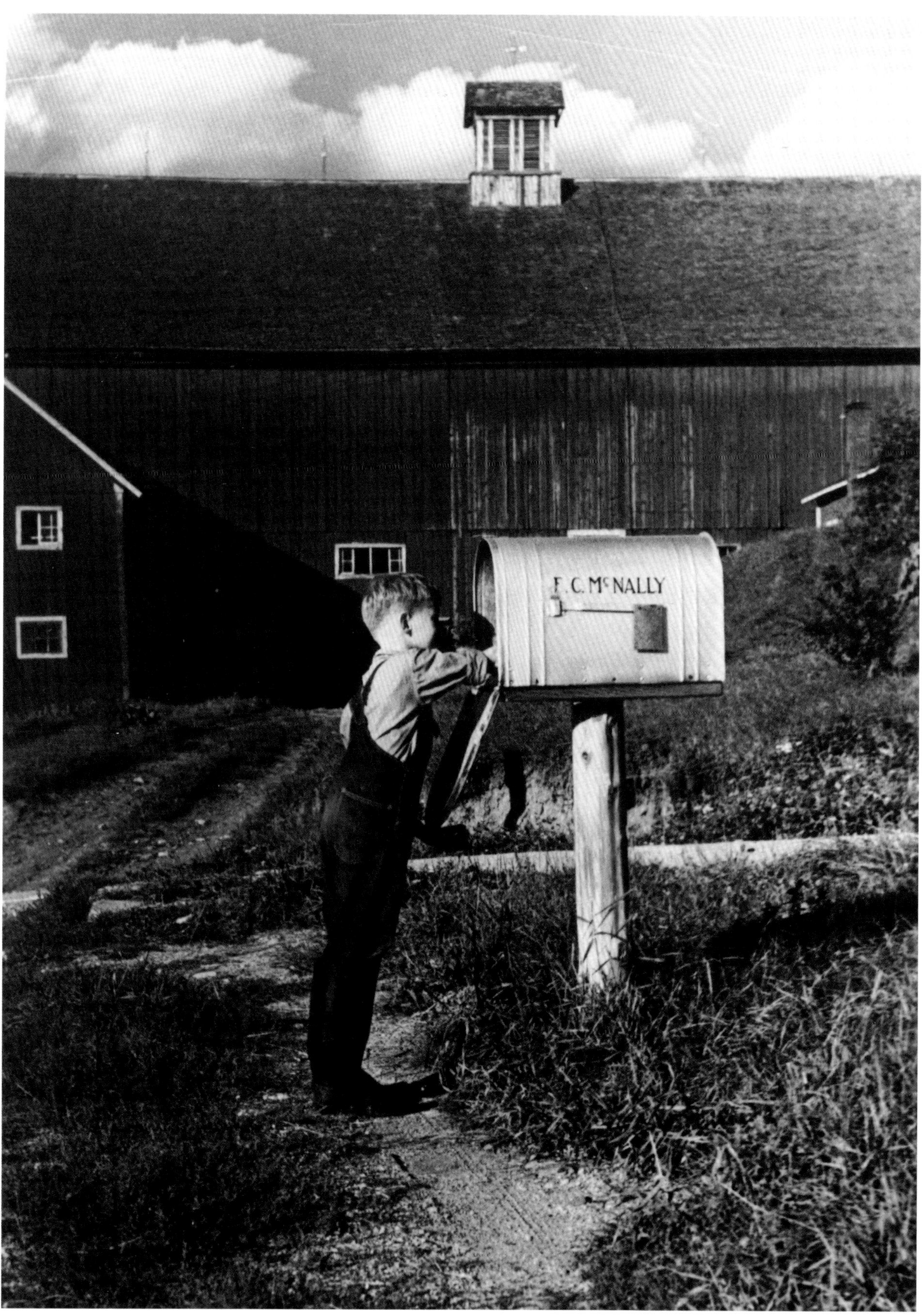
C. McNALLY

Rothstein never regretted the years he spent on the road with the Historical Section. Unlike Mydans, who found a quality of sameness that bound Americans together, Rothstein discovered—after years spent criss-crossing the country on the government's behalf—that the Americans he had met were distinguished by their individualism. "One thing I found in traveling through the United States was that every man and every woman was different," he said in an interview years later. "I found that a kind of individualism existed among the people, an inability to conform, a desire to be the master of their own fate."[20] This tenacity and stubbornness became a part of his portrait of Vermont.

NOTES

1 / Ellis.

2 / O'Neal, p. 22.

3 / Soule to Stryker, 12 June 1937.

4 / Stryker and Wood, p. 3.

5 / Rothstein interview, p. 2.

6 / Hurley, *Portrait of a Decade*, p. 82.

7 / Rothstein interview, p. 9.

8 / FSA archive, Library of Congress.

9 / O'Neal, p. 21.

10 / Curtis, p. 75.

11 / Stryker to Falke, 10 August 1937.

12 / Stryker to Russell Lee, 24 September 1937.

13 / Stryker to Lange, 30 September 1937.

14 / Rosskams interview, p. 10.

15 / Rothstein interview, p. 10.

16 / Locke to Stryker, 4 September 1937.

17 / Stryker to Russell Lee, 1 November 1937.

18 / Stryker to Pope, 6 April 1940.

19 / Edwin Locke to Harold J. Ruttenberg, 18 July 1938. Ruttenberg was research director of the Steel Workers Organizing Committee.

20 / Rothstein interview, p. 28.

1938

No Historical Section photographer made an official visit to the state during 1938, but Roy Stryker traveled to southern Vermont in late April at the invitation of Bennington College President Robert Leigh. Leigh had asked the chief of the Historical Section to give a lecture to a photography class. It was perhaps a class taught by Professor James L. McCamy, who had written to Stryker five months earlier explaining that he was writing a dissertation on government publicity. McCamy wanted to include a chapter on the kind of work being undertaken by the Historical Section. His letter contains an astute summary of the Historical Section's emerging style:

> I have a section on photography in a chapter on the use of media. It concludes that the RA [Resettlement Administration] type of thing is the emerging pattern that should be followed by all agencies dealing with subjects that need to be forcibly planted in the national vocabulary. It attempts a description of your stuff in terms of warmth, intimacy, dramatic impact, and the use of persons anonymously to symbolize large conditions.[1]

As the winter passed, Stryker, Leigh, and McCamy continued to correspond. Leigh had advice to offer about how Stryker should develop his talk: "My only suggestion is that you stay off 'Art' and talk about photography as documentation and as a medium of information, education, publicity, propaganda, or whatever word you prefer to use for 'publicity.' You know as well as I how little can be accomplished in talking to artists on such a debatable subject." Leigh also conceded that it would be difficult to look at the pictures that would accompany Stryker's lecture purely as documentation. "Of course your exhibit will be damned good art and will be recognized as such," he wrote, "but I know from experience that a social studies speaker is always more impressive if he stays off of esthetics."[2] These directives played directly to Stryker's own vision of the work the Historical Section was doing; namely, that its photographs should document the full range of the rural American scene with pictures combining sociology and aesthetics.

For his part, Stryker was happy to accept an invitation to visit a state he loved. In early April, just before he came north for the lecture, he expressed to McCamy how much he was looking forward to escaping Washington. "Vermont always soothes my nerves anyway," he wrote. "Migod, how I envy you the peace and quiet (I suppose you do have peace and quiet up there) of the Vermont hills."[3]

The lecture became the occasion for what may have been the only exhibit of Historical Section photographs in Vermont during the years of the section's active work. Unfortunately, no other record of the lecture or the exhibit has been uncovered. However, they had at least one result. According to a letter McCamy wrote to Stryker in late June, the photography students who attended the lecture received an assignment at the next class to take their cameras into the field to try to duplicate the Historical Section's type of photography. McCamy wrote:

> They went around Vermont for some time trying to emulate your stuff, with, I might add, little success, though they were excited over the idea and annoyed that they couldn't immediately grasp the insight and perception required for good documentary.[4]

In the same letter McCamy asked for copies of Historical Section photographs to illustrate his dissertation. He reiterated his interpretation of the kind of work the Historical Section was attempting as it integrated the theories Stryker had developed at Columbia, the style of Walker Evans, and the government's needs:

> Some of [the Historical Section's photography] characteristics cited in the text are its intimate approach to human beings as symbols of economic conditions, its relation of persons to their environment especially when the land is a part of their environment, and its quality of taking the meaningful item to represent a whole.[5]

That summer Stryker went to his cottage on Lake Eden, attempting to escape the summer heat in Washington and hoping, as he had in the past, to enjoy some quiet with his wife and young daughter. However, threats of a budget cut forced him to cut his vacation short and take the night train back to Washington. He knew, as perhaps no one else did, that only his vigilance and his forceful personality could continue to save a program that in his eyes was only getting launched.[6]

NOTES

1 / McCamy to Stryker, 5 December 1937.

2 / Leigh to Stryker, 1 February 1938.

3 / Stryker to McCamy, 12 April 1938.

4 / McCamy to Stryker, 26 June 1938.

5 / Ibid.

6 / Stryker interview, p. 28.

Russell Lee

Two years passed after Arthur Rothstein made his third, and most important, trip to Vermont before another Historical Section photographer visited the state. Russell Lee (fig. 10) arrived in October 1939, and worked his way up from the southwest corner of the state, following Route 7 north from Bennington to Rutland. After making his way, probably along Route 4, to Bridgewater, he continued east to Woodstock, and from there he made his way north to Bradford, almost thirty miles up the Connecticut River from White River Junction. It was a short trip of several weeks, and the assignment was not broad but focused, much like Rothstein's assignment in April 1937 for the Agricultural Adjustment Administration.

Unlike many of the other Historical Section photographers who enjoyed taking pictures of all sorts of people, objects, and activities, knowing that Stryker would manage to find homes for their work in the broad category of the American scene, Lee liked doing file work, addressing the specific themes formulated in Stryker's active imagination. Trained as a chemical engineer at Lehigh University, he worked for four years as a plant manager for Certainteed Products, but the work bored him. He resigned in 1929 and spent the next two years studying painting at the California School of Fine Arts. Armed with skills that better suited his temperament, he went to New York to paint and study further under John Sloan. Eventually, however, frustration with his drafting skills drove him to seek accuracy of visual representation with a Contax 35mm camera. After a brief spell in Woodstock, New York, with his first wife, Doris, who was a cousin of artist Ben Shahn and also an artist, Lee took his camera on the road to photograph bootleg coal-mining operations in Pennsylvania and streetscapes in New York City and Woodstock. These comprised the portfolio he took to Washington in the early summer of 1936 to show to Roy Stryker. Stryker was impressed, but had no openings. Discouraged, Lee went back to Woodstock, but within a month Stryker had summoned him to take some photographs in New Jersey. While Lee was in Washington delivering the negatives to Stryker, Carl Mydans signaled his intention to resign. Stryker invited Lee to take his place.

Unlike most of the other photographers who worked for the Historical Section, Lee had some independent means. He worked as hard as anyone on the staff and spent his nights on the road in the same kinds of humble surroundings that everyone else in the section endured on the government's per diem of five dollars. However, his family money enabled him to buy excellent equipment to supplement that supplied by the Historical Section. To enhance his work, he purchased a Super Ikonta B camera that made outstanding 2¼ × 2¼-inch negatives and had flash synchronization that made it perfect for the interior work he enjoyed. He also purchased a larger 3¼ × 4¼-inch press-type camera to add to the government-supplied Contax.[1]

FIGURE 10
Portrait of Russell Lee, FSA photographer. 1942.

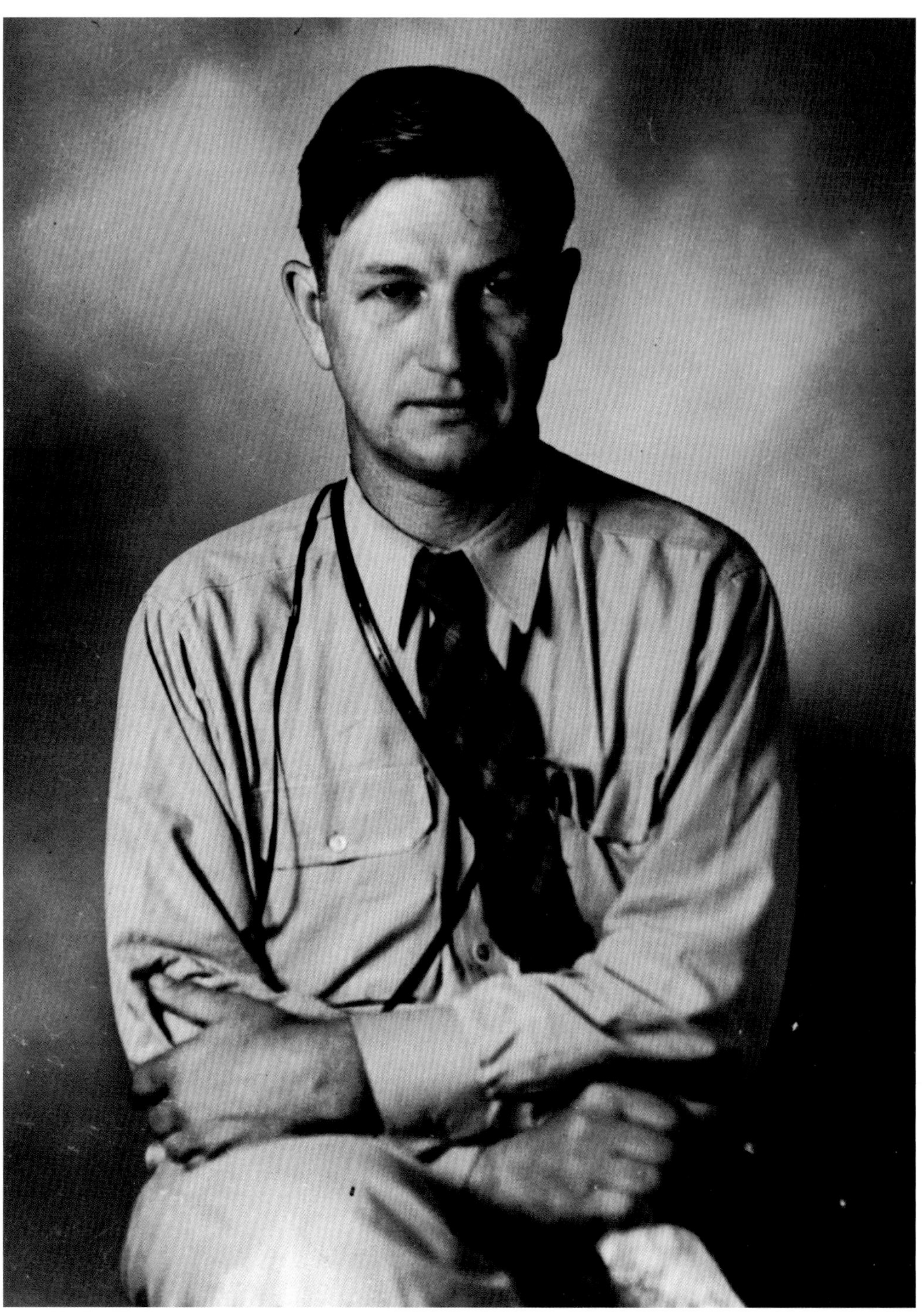

Lee's first assignment was in his Midwest homeland. Sent out for six weeks, he stayed for nine months, establishing the pattern of the long-distance relationship that would distinguish his tenure with the section. No other Historical Section photographer would travel more miles on its behalf; no other photographer would contribute as many photographs to its file; no other photographer would stay as long; and no other photographer would establish the kind of friendships within the section that Lee enjoyed. With Rothstein, the rapport was professional. Both were trained in science and interested in the technical side of photography. They improved the darkroom facilities in Washington and experimented with cameras, even to the point of trying to invent improved flash units. With Stryker, the friendship was intensely personal. The two men wrote regularly while Lee was on the road, and the letters were intimate exchanges that went beyond what was necessary to accomplish the section's work.

Lee arrived in Vermont near the middle of October 1939.[2] He was traveling with Harold Ballou, who a month later would join Stryker in northern New England on what Stryker called "purely a reconnaissance trip" to "formulate a lot of new ideas as to how to approach this New England problem."[3] Ballou's reasons for accompanying Lee in October of 1939 are unknown, but at least one of them was personal. The two men made a stop at a cemetery in Quechee, outside Woodstock, where Lee took a photograph of Ballou standing at the graves of some of his ancestors. Lee noted the photograph on his caption sheet, but it does not exist in the Vermont file. His notes suggest that Ballou kept it.[4]

The photographs Lee took on his only trip to Vermont defy easy classification: farms, barns, homes, a graveyard, a historical marker, a railroad crossing, a stone quarry, a battery-powered radio, and mileage and directional signs. A number of these subjects convey the idea that Americans possessed the technology in the prewar years to be connected as a nation, an idea Stryker enthusiastically promoted. However, they are also scenes and artifacts that define rural America in the 1930s, each one capturing a piece of the soul of a place, and none of them conveying it entirely. This was how Roy Stryker envisioned the work of the Historical Section. He imagined a collection of tens of thousands of prints that together would create a portrait of the United States during the depression. He thought only in terms of the complete file. When photographers managed from time to time to take a single photograph of surpassing beauty or compelling emotion, he was delighted, but the image was no more or less important than thousands of others in the file. Within this amplitude, even photographs of mundane subjects had their place. In this light, Lee's photograph of a historical marker in Woodstock became part of a collection of photographs about Vermont that portray a rural state with a sturdy population, a distinguished history, and often striking scenery. Lee understood Stryker's vision of the file perhaps better than any of the other section photographers and was happy to contribute. Years afterward, looking back at what the section had accomplished, Lee said:

> We were just interested in building a file which would show just about, well, everything there was; as a matter of fact, I used this historical thing in approaching people. I was a member of the Historical Section, and whenever they asked me, "What are you doing out here taking pictures?" I said, "Well, I'm taking pictures of the history of today." And they understood this.[5]

Lee's assignment took him to the area around Bradford, where he brought together his skill, enthusiasms, and empathy for those who, unlike him, did not have independent means with which to support themselves. Apparently the task was to photograph several Farm Security Administration clients in Bradford; in doing so he produced some of the most moving images of Vermont taken in the 1930s (fig. 11). Much of the work brought him from the outdoors to the indoors, where he preferred to work, because he believed interiors reveal a great deal more about people than exteriors.[6] The move indoors also put him

FIGURE 11 (opposite)
Russell Lee
Bradford (vicinity), Orange County, Vt. October 1939. Fall scene on a farm. Notice the hay in the mow and the sleigh before the door.

in intimate contact with several FSA families and challenged him technically. The results are startling and deeply disturbing. Lee's photographs suggest that some of the families pressed by the depression in Vermont were managing to hold their own. Although the interiors are shabby, the children are clean and there is food on the table and more food stored in the cellars. In other pictures, however, a young girl scrounges at a kitchen table surrounded by squalor, and dirty children amuse themselves amid peeling wallpaper with the merest of playthings. The line between those who are succeeding and those who are not is indistinct but detectable, and the difference is more than moving; it is heartbreaking.

Lee excelled at the type of photography that was both documentary and social commentary. Warm and outgoing, he found it easy to win his subjects' trust, but he did not do so by softening any of the edges of their circumstances. Rather he relied on a flat flash to illuminate everything in the room equally. The effect, according to Louise Rosskam, a photographer and the wife of another Historical Section employee, was to "eliminate all possible atmosphere, so that the picture becomes a bare, brutal kind of inventory of poverty."[7] Illuminated by an unforgiving light, the images are stark and shocking, richly detailed, and carefully composed. In one, a young girl plays in front of an old fireplace, with paint and wallpaper peel around her; but framed above the mantle is a floral poster that says "God Bless Our Home," and beside that is a small oval print of George Washington (fig. 12).

The depth of this series about poverty gives substance to an admonition Stryker gave Lee more than two years earlier to shoot more pictures of one family rather than more families.[8] Stryker had, in fact, two different kinds of photographic techniques in mind. "I would suggest that you do as you have done in the past," he advised Lee in a letter dated 3 April 1937. "Use two different methods; first, that of a scattered method—many pictures of similar types of cases and people; second, the case method on two or three outstanding or interesting families."[9] Lee's series of approximately three dozen photographs of three anonymous families shows powerfully and poignantly how inescapable their poverty was. It moved with them through the day, through their activities and through their home, pervading every aspect and minute of their lives.

The question inevitably arises, Why did people permit themselves to be photographed in these circumstances? Those receiving some sort of federal aid probably felt they had no choice. Beyond that, Stryker said that Lee possessed the ability "to move into an area quietly and emerge a few days later with pictures that showed he had been completely accepted as a member of the community. His work often had a friendly 'family album' quality," surely an ironic description considering the cultural and economic gulf that separated Lee and his subjects.[10] Just as importantly, Lee and the other Historical Section photographers felt tremendous empathy for their subjects. Much of the success of their photographs can be attributed to their passionate commitment to treat the people they photographed with the utmost dignity. As evidence, the Historical Section files are replete with images of people shown in the context of their lives and accomplishments, people tied together across economic, social, and cultural classes by their ordinary humanity: parents with their children, families and their homes, fathers and mothers engaged in their work.

Beyond this, as the photographers discovered, the poor often wanted their stories told because they believed that if knowledge of their desperate straits were widespread, Americans or the government would reach out to help them. One elderly farmer even gave Lee a nickel after being photographed, because he thought the work was important and he wanted to contribute.[11]

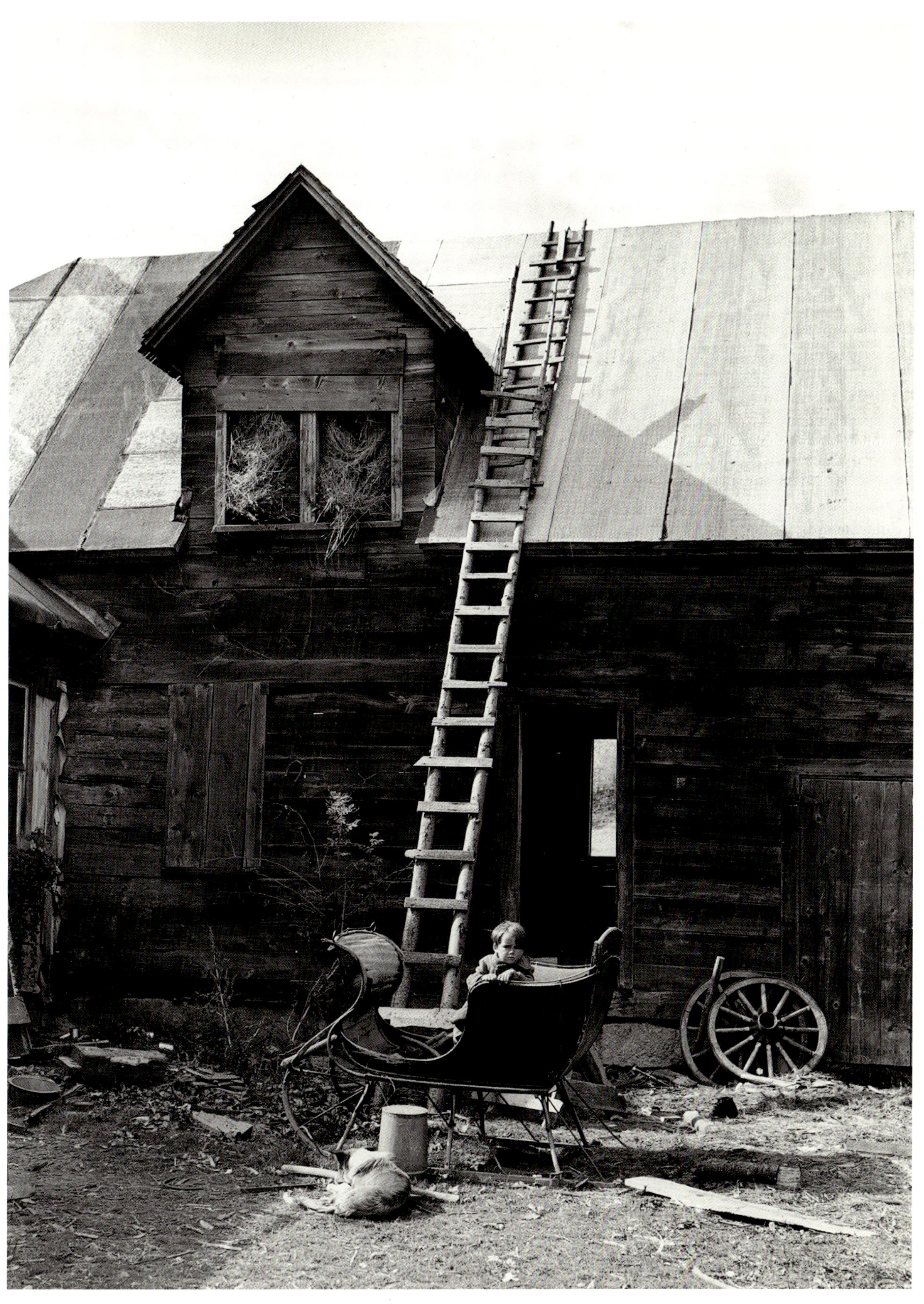

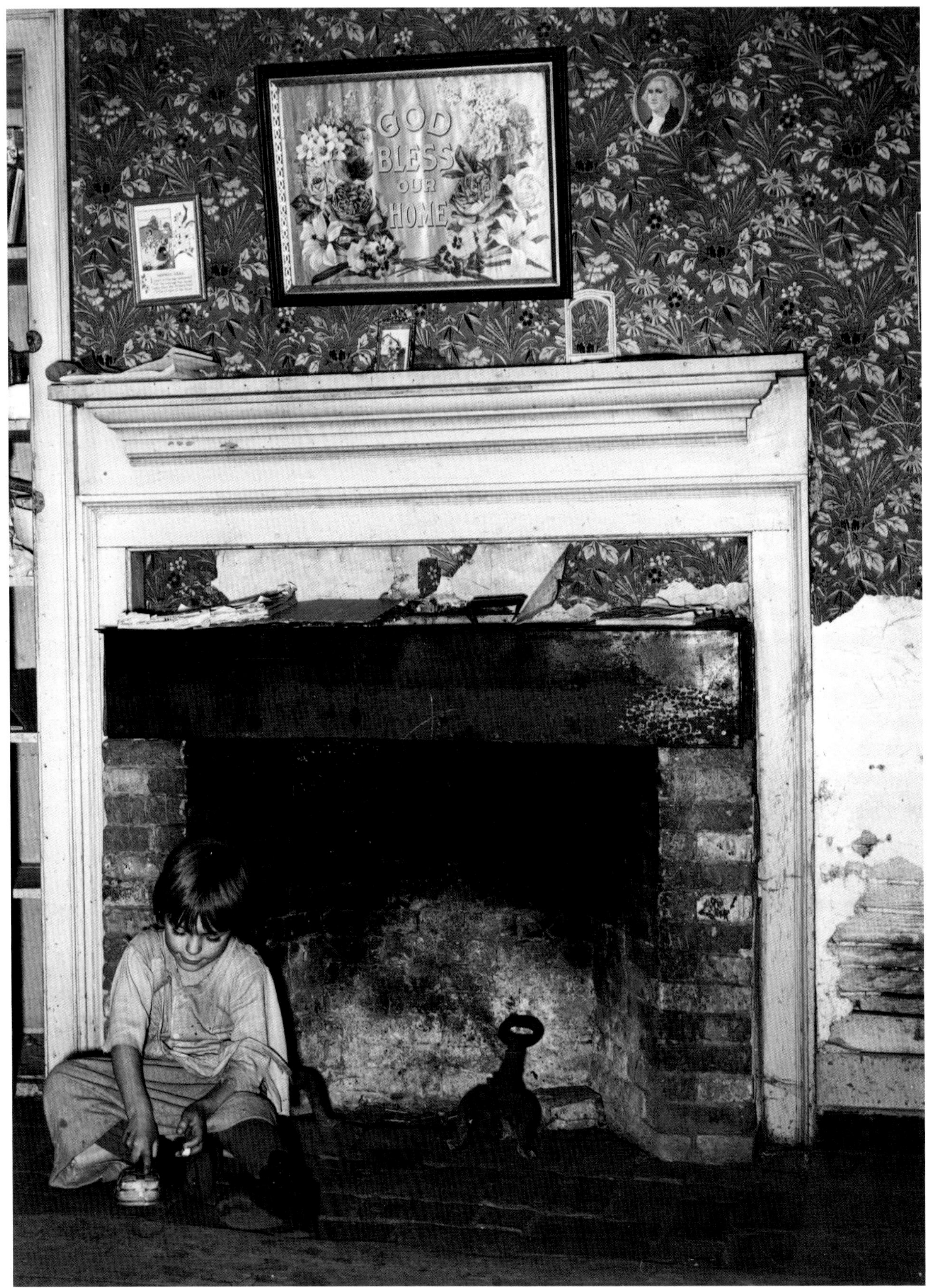
GOD
BLESS
OUR
HOME

FIGURE 12 (opposite)
Russell Lee
Bradford, Orange County (vicinity), Vt. October 1939. Fireplace in the farm home of an FSA client.

The work was a gamble, however. Photographs like the most poignant of the Bradford series could inspire ridicule as easily as empathy. Stryker was aware of this. In the late winter of 1940, he wrote to Lee:

> Every so often, I am brought to a realization of the ruthlessness of the camera, particularly the way we have been using it. A lot of those people whose picture you took do not realize how they are going to look in the eyes of smug, smart city people when these pictures are reproduced. Of course, we could turn right around, and put the camera on the smug, smart city people, and make them look ridiculous, too.[12]

But of course, that was outside the purview of the Historical Section. Only one section photographer, Marion Post, tried to photograph the wealthy. She took her camera to Florida one winter and went to the racetrack, among other upper-class places. Unlike most of the poor, who viewed the Historical Section photographers on their doorsteps with skepticism but rarely with hostility, the well-turned-out gamblers had her escorted from the track and confiscated her film.[13] Stryker's vision of a file that broadly represented the American scene in the late 1930s and early 1940s was consequently thwarted, both by the narrower scope of his government assignment and by the reluctance of the middle and upper class to expose their own vulnerabilities in a national photography project that was attracting increasing attention. Thus it remained the poor, who had little to lose, who were willing to risk their dignity in the hope of improving their lives.

The seemingly endless stream of images of poverty and despair, however, sometimes took a toll on the section photographers, particularly on the most sensitive ones. Lee, who was known for his sensitivity, from time to time simply had to turn away from all the suffering he encountered. At those moments, he stowed his Contax and looked to landscapes and townscapes for emotional and aesthetic relief.[14] This may explain the pictures he shot in Bradford (home to some of the FSA clients he portrayed) of young boys raking leaves or a street scene with a remarkable line of stately elm trees that unmistakably allude to the capacity of living things to endure.

Lee stayed with the Historical Section until it dissolved in 1942 into the Office of War Information. Through all his years with the section he lived on the road, stopping in Washington no more than one month a year and keeping to his routine of shooting four magazines of film each day (for a total of forty-eight to sixty photographs) on the Speed Graphic camera and loading new magazines every night.[15] Every three or four days he sought out a hotel with a bathroom that he could convert into a darkroom. After the film was developed, he captioned the negatives and sent the parcel off to Washington. Jean, his second wife, whom he had met while on the road, almost always accompanied him after 1938, taking notes for captions and distracting people with conversation so their portraits would be less self-conscious. The series of Historical Section photographs for which he became best known was shot after his sojourn to Vermont. In hundreds of images he captured of Pietown, New Mexico, he portrayed the intricacies and intimacies of daily life in a culturally complex small town.

Lee completed another important project two years after his visit to Vermont. This took him out of the countryside and put him in city ghettos with Richard Wright, who had proposed a book about the despair of urban blacks. Wright turned to the Historical Section for help assembling photographs as illustrations. Lee enthusiastically participated, visiting black slums in Chicago and recording the poverty he found there, which was at least as wrenching as the rural poverty he had encountered on the road for the Historical Section. When *Twelve Million Black Voices* was published in 1941, Lee's work accounted for one-fifth of the photographs.[16]

Life on the road was difficult, but Lee preferred it to being desk-bound. He loved taking photographs and he loved to travel. His response to people who asked him why he wanted to photograph them revealed how passionately he believed that photography could serve as a form of communication to spread understanding to the nation's distant corners: "I want to show people in other parts of the country how you live."[17] His photographs of Vermont, revealing the squalor and desperation of the poor, are among the most extraordinary images taken by Historical Section photographers in the state. The poignant message they sent was compelling evidence that the nation's most needy were not confined to the drought-stricken Midwest. However, looking back years later, Lee said that he discovered during those years with the Historical Section the nation's "real basic strength" and a spirit of pride and optimism that was indomitable.[18]

NOTES

1 / Lee, *Russell Lee,* p. 17.

2 / Lee to Stryker, 9 October 1939.

3 / Stryker to Lee, 3 November 1939.

4 / FSA archive, Library of Congress.

5 / Lees interview, p. 28.

6 / O'Neal, p. 138.

7 / Rosskams interview, p. 31.

8 / Stryker to Lee, 19 January 1937.

9 / Stryker to Lee, 3 April 1937.

10 / Hurley, *Portrait of a Decade,* p. 78.

11 / Lees interview, p. 29.

12 / Stryker to Lee, 19 March 1940.

13 / Post Wolcott interview, p. 16.

14 / Lee, *Russell Lee,* p. 19.

15 / Lees interview, p. 10.

16 / Lee, *Russell Lee,* p. 20.

17 / Lee, "Life on the American Frontier."

18 / Lees interview, p. 30.

Marion Post

During one of the discouraging hiatuses when the Historical Section's fluctuating fortunes forced Roy Stryker to suspend Dorothea Lange's work with the agency, Lange wrote to him that "I guess being a Resettlement photographer is not a woman's job."[1] No one ever convinced Marion Post of that, however. When she arrived in Vermont in February 1940, she was a veteran of eighteen months on the road for the section (fig. 13). She had learned from painful experience how to dress conservatively enough not to offend the people she was sent to record, why she had to approach all situations involving African American men with caution to avoid imperiling their lives, and how to fend off unwanted advances from sheriffs, farmers, traveling salesmen, bureaucrats, and government officials, some of whom occasionally accompanied her on assignment. She had not lost her high spirits, however. Vermont in winter was exciting country to Post, who had spent some time there as a child, and she was looking forward to the assignment.

Born into an affluent family that was divided politically, Post was sent to boarding school at thirteen when her parents divorced. Thereafter, she generally followed her mother's liberal interests.[2] After graduating from high school, she took courses in anthropology and dance at the New School for Social Research, and eventually enrolled at New York University to study educational psychology. Throughout school and after she left the university, she taught young children at progressive schools in New York and Massachusetts, growing increasingly disturbed at the socio-economic divisions she observed in her classrooms. Her older sister, living in Vienna, persuaded Post to join her in Europe and take classes, first in Berlin and later at the University of Vienna. While in Europe, she purchased her first camera and began taking photographs. According to an interview she gave decades later, the camera techniques she learned in Europe, particularly how to use available light, were more advanced than those currently used in the United States.[3]

Eventually the tensions preceding the outbreak of war in Europe drove both sisters home. Post accepted another teaching assignment, but she moonlighted by selling photographs she took with her Rollei, a small, compact, twin-lens reflex camera. She joined the progressive New York Photo League and a small tutorial with the photographer Ralph Steiner. When he encouraged her, she started to market her photographs to wire services and to magazines such as *Fortune*, *Survey Graphic*, and the *New York Times Magazine*.[4] Success prompted her to quit teaching and take a job as a photographer with the *Philadelphia Evening Bulletin*. At the newspaper she learned how to take photographs in difficult circumstances and how to cope with male chauvinism in the workplace, lessons that would come in handy in her government work.[5]

The *Evening Bulletin* offered a good education, but Post found fashion photography for the women's pages unsatisfying. After eighteen months at the paper, she went in search of work that "was more useful or had more purpose to it."[6] At Steiner's suggestion, she

FIGURE 13
Arthur Rothstein
Marion Post with Rolleiflex and Speed Graffic in hand in Montgomery County, Maryland. 1940.

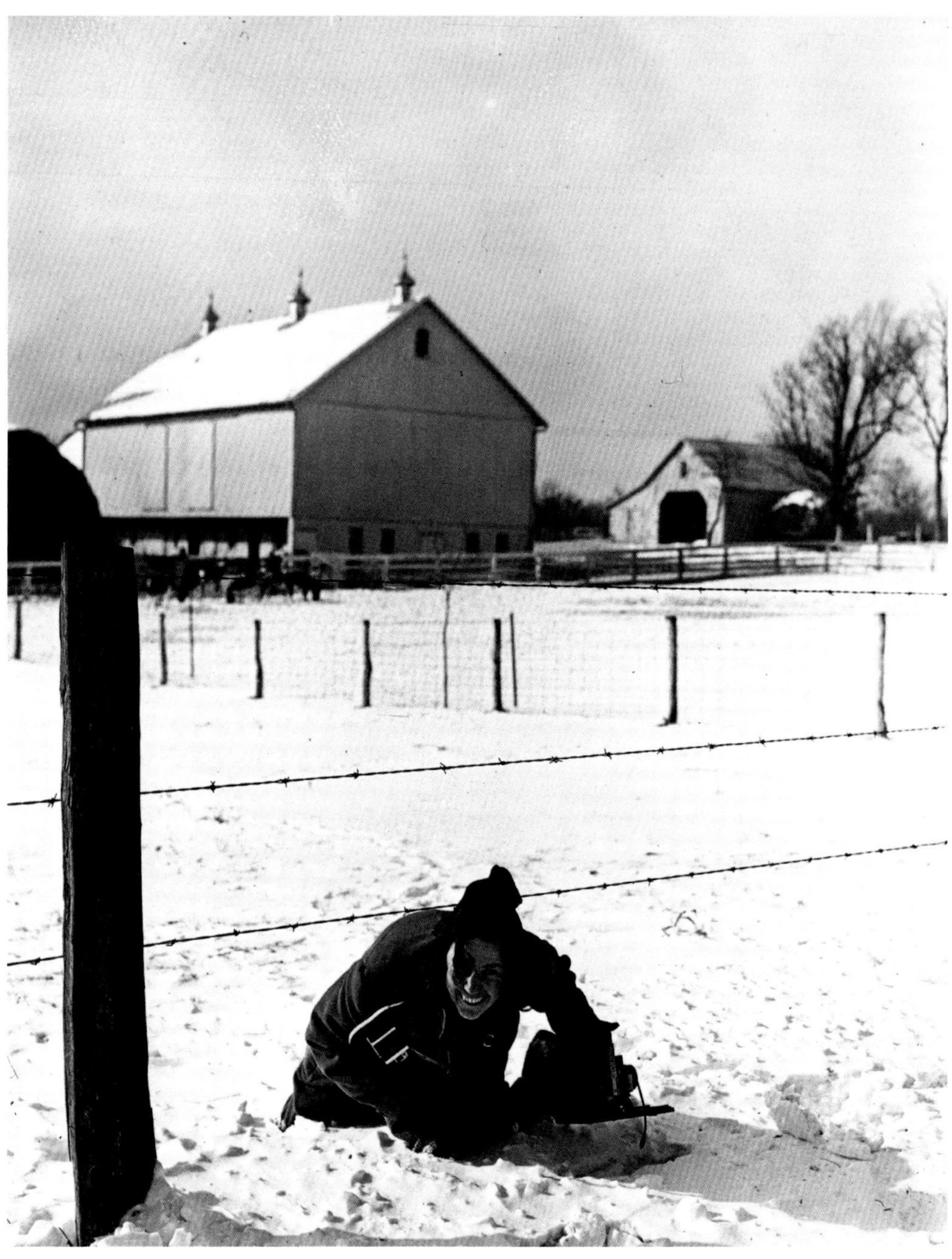

assembled a portfolio of her work that he personally took to Stryker. Encouraged by Stryker's response, she put together a broader portfolio and went to Washington herself with a letter of introduction from well-known photographer Paul Strand, in which he recommended her as a "young photographer of considerable experience who has made a number of very good photographs on social themes in the South and elsewhere."[7] While Stryker assessed Post's work, Post studied the photographs in the file; each came away impressed.[8] Stryker hired the twenty-five-year-old photographer on a three-month trial at the standard rate: $2,300 per year, $5 per day for expenses on the road, and $.045 per mile. Although not generous terms, they were adequate and similar to those offered to her coworkers. Also like them, Post would receive film, flashbulbs, and miscellaneous other

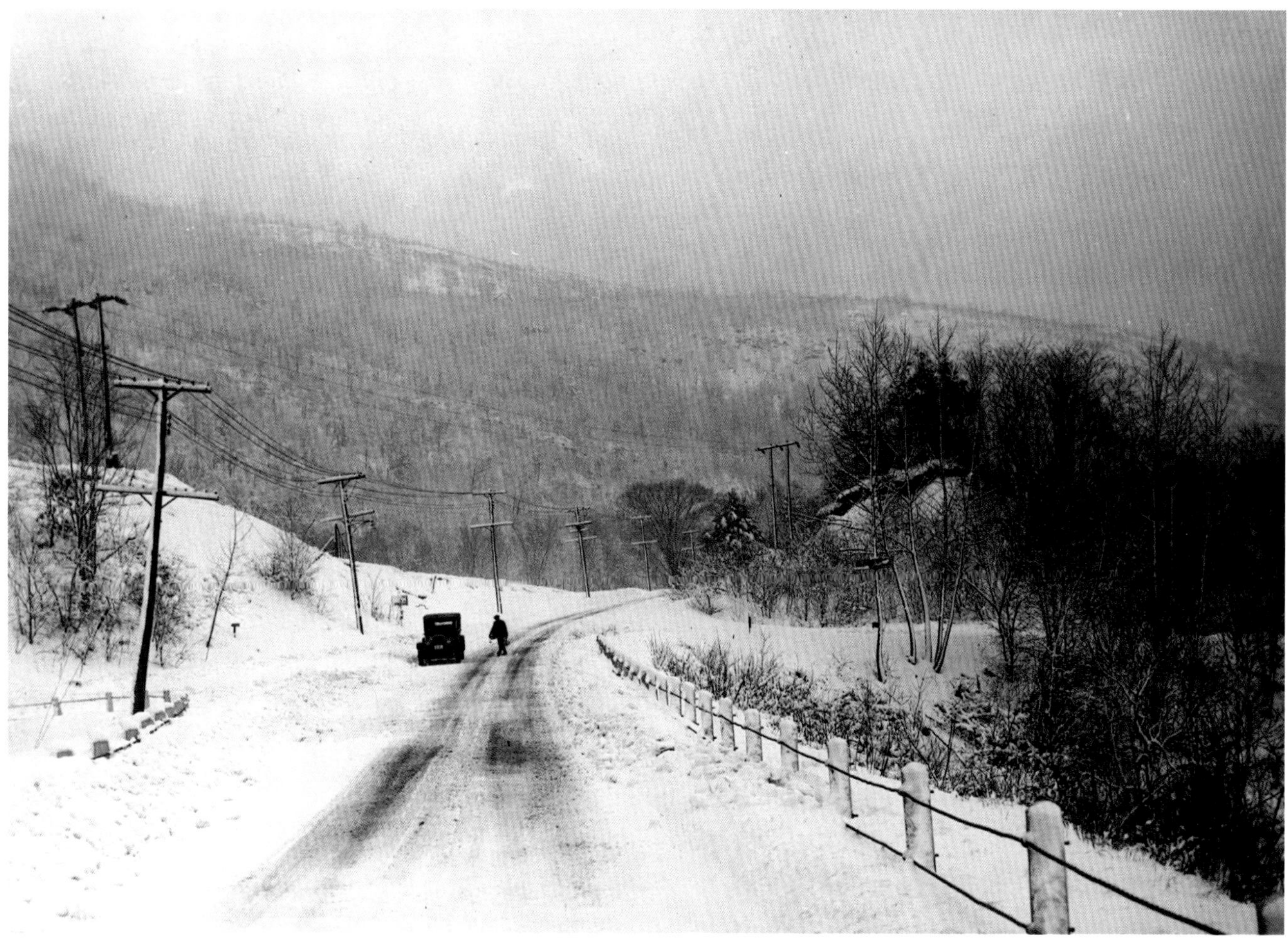

FIGURE 14
Marion Post Wolcott
Brattleboro (vicinity), Vt. March 1940. Highway after a blizzard.

equipment, but would be expected to supply her own special cameras. "However," added Stryker, "it is our desire to standardize as far as possible on the Leica, Contax, and 3¼ × 4¼ Speed Graphic."[9]

Post joined the Historical Section when it was at a crossroads. Most of the early photographers—Evans, Mydans, and Lange—had already left the section to pursue other work. The two who were left—Arthur Rothstein and Russell Lee—had survived the fluctuating budgets over the past three years and were dogged, indefatigable photographers committed to the ever-expanding file. Month after month, they had shown themselves willing to live on the road, to endure difficult living and working conditions, and to photograph the sorts of grim scenes that the Farm Security Administration and the Resettlement Administration were intent on ameliorating with their national programs and education. By mid-1938, however, Stryker had decided that the file contained enough scenes of misery to make that point. Moreover, he thought the file contained too few images of the landscapes, family, town, and civic scenes that portrayed America's strengths. He was gradually but inexorably expanding the scope of the file to capture America's "other" side.

By the time Post arrived in Vermont in late February 1940, she had proven herself in a number of ways. Her photographs of West Virginia coal miners satisfied Stryker and others that she had the mettle to handle herself in stressful situations. She had learned the hard way that her bright clothing, slacks, and long hair generally gave the poor people she was sent to photograph the wrong idea about her, and that she would need to adjust her presentation to their more conservative natures.[10] She also had established herself as a photographer who took both sensitive pictures of people and evocative pictures of the land. She took some ribbing for taking "beautiful pictures of the good earth"—she herself referred to the pictures as "cheesecake"—but her passion for the land's beauty was genuine.[11] So was her interest in trying to portray New England in winter.

Post probably entered Vermont through its southeast corner and came up Route 5, stopping in Guilford, Brattleboro, Putney, Bellows Falls, West Hartford, and Hartford. The photographs she took of highways, towns, and roadside farms blanketed in snow are moody, stirring evocations of the good earth asleep. In that regard, they are a departure from other Historical Section photographs taken in Vermont. Post, however, felt that winter offered a unique advantage over other seasons to photographers trying to capture a region's geography and character. "Winter is the only time to photograph farms and towns, really locating them in their relation to the land and mountains," she wrote to Stryker from New Hampshire soon after she had left Vermont.[12]

Moreover, according to Edwin Rosskam, who often wrote the shooting scripts for the Historical Section photographers, the themes were expanding, and winter itself became a theme. "I remember sending Marion out to do a coverage of winter. Well, it must have been a twenty-page shooting script of that," he recalled decades later.[13] Post welcomed the challenge of working in winter and of trying to portray something of the region's character, as she knew it. "Nobody had done anything of snow or cold except some of [John] Vachon's pictures later on of the blizzards in the West, but very little had been done in the file," she recalled in 1965. "There was very little in the file at the time of New England and that kind of ruggedness, and . . . of course, I had visited New England as a child off and on all my life."[14]

The weather soon provided all the challenge she could hope for (figs. 14 and 15). On 19 February Post wrote to Stryker in one of her regular eight-to-ten page handwritten letters, "Obliging juicy blizzard. Tough going. . . . Staying Brattleboro Tonight. Farther North Tomorrow."[15] Delayed by the storm, she needed five days to reach Woodstock and make some friends who were willing to introduce her to several local farmers. When she finally made contact, however, she had more than Yankee reserve to contend with. "I've had a lot to learn these first days about caring for a car in this bitter cold and learning about driving and managing it on these icy snowy rutty roads," she admitted to Stryker. "It's been below zero every morning—from 10 to 20, sometimes terribly cold and grey all day, and one day or so with intermittent sunshine. Indoors it's most often just about as cold as outside except for one or two rooms." She was undaunted by the circumstances, however. Almost certainly trying to make Stryker blush, she concluded with, "What really ruins my disposition are the icy cold toilet seats."[16]

She expected to be busy, and she was, but the conditions were nearly overwhelming. When her tripod kept sinking in the snow, she improvised by putting ski pole baskets on its legs. When she kept sinking in snowdrifts, she bought snowshoes. Other problems were not solved as easily: "Shall I even try to tell you the difficulties I ran into with equipment when the temperature was so low everything stuck and just refused to operate at least half the time. Shutters, diaphragms, range finders, tracks, film and magazine slides become so brittle they just snap in two."[17] Desperate to coax her cameras to work, she began wrapping them with hot water bottles or tucking them into her car engine near the heater.[18]

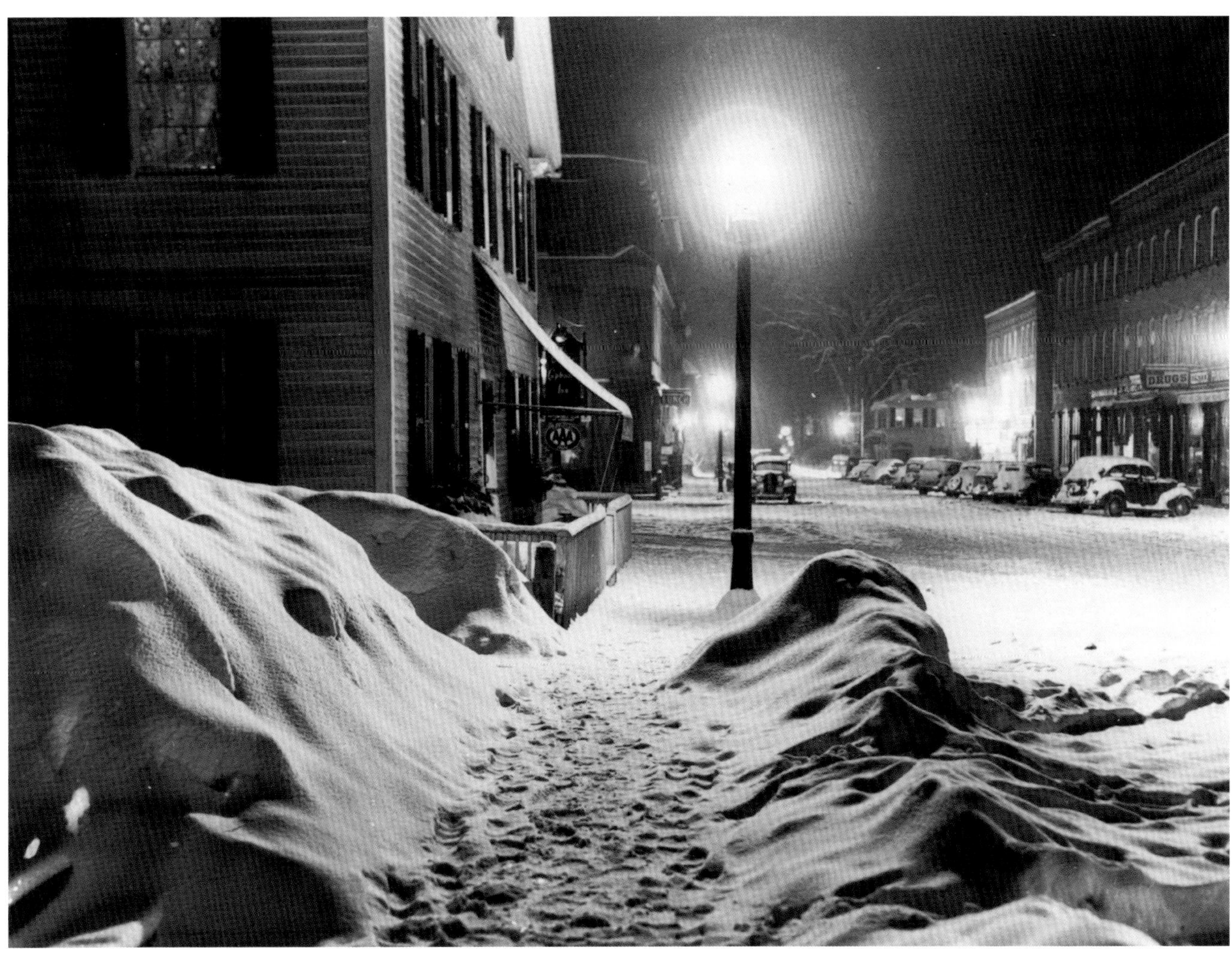

FIGURE 15

Marion Post Wolcott

Woodstock, Vt. March 1940.

Center of town.

Once she solved the logistical problems, she began photographing giant icicles hanging from eaves, children sledding and throwing snowballs, people making their way cautiously down sidewalks narrowed to footpaths by snow banks, and houses buried in snow up to their windowsills. To illustrate how New Englanders coped with the frigid temperatures and a two-month drought, she took pictures of farmers carrying buckets of water to their cattle. She took an extended series of photographs of a peddler who made his way by sleigh from one Vermont town to another (fig. 16). She took dozens of photographs of Woodstock's historic houses buried beneath snow, and unwittingly captured that town on the cusp of becoming a glamorous tourist attraction, ferried into the second half of the twentieth century by America's nostalgic search for its heritage and the growing rage for skiing. Perhaps remembering an admonition from Stryker early in her association with the Historical Section that it would be better to take a few good photographs than to photograph everything in sight, she now felt obliged to explain to her boss why she was taking so many photographs. "You will find many duplicates too," she wrote to Stryker from Woodstock, "because I took things several times hoping the shutter would eventually, or just once, work reasonably well."[19]

Very quickly, however, she realized that she would need extra time with this assignment and that Woodstock was not a typical Vermont town. "I want to go to another smaller town that doesn't have all the background of wealth that this one does," she wrote to Stryker.[20] And he agreed on both scores. "By all means take the necessary time that you are going to need to do a good job. It is, after all, terribly important. It is our first chance to do

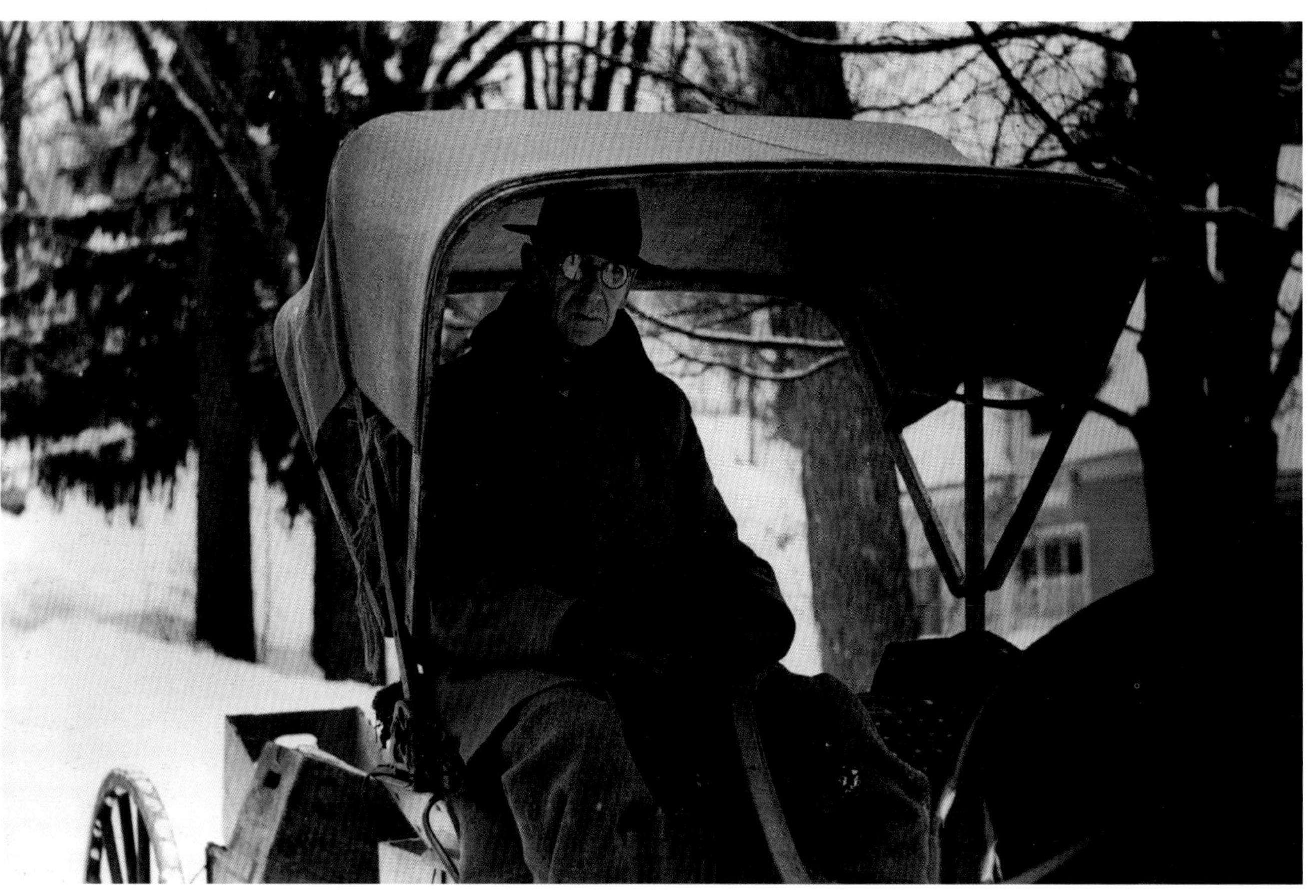

FIGURE 16
Marion Post Wolcott
Woodstock, Vt. March 1940. Old fashioned country peddler who goes from door to door selling hardware and groceries.

real good winter scenes, and New England has been pretty much neglected, as far as our files are concerned," he wrote back. He went on to offer advice based on firsthand knowledge of Woodstock. "Woodstock is a lovely town. We have been through there many times, and stayed there a couple of nights. . . .You are going to find a lot of small towns, not far away, which will probably give you a little more of the atmosphere which you want."[21] That same day, Stryker sent what he called a "Weekly Gossip Sheet" to Lee, Post, and Rothstein in which he mentioned that Post was getting good photographs of "winter in the town and winter on the farm."[22]

Before Post left Woodstock, she took two significant series of photographs. One was only remotely related to the weather. Rather, it concerned a book titled *Home Town*, from a series called The Face of America, in which Sherwood Anderson proposed to examine those aspects of the nation's culture that were uniquely American and thereby to calm Americans' jitters in the face of events unfolding in Europe. Anderson proposed using Historical Section photographs to illustrate the text, and Stryker loved the idea of assembling a series of photographs that would capture the spirit, traditions, and resilience of rural America. When Post proposed staying in Woodstock through Town Meeting Day in early March to do a series of photographs of the town gathering, Stryker replied enthusiastically: "We wish you luck. What an addition that will be to our files and to the small town book."[23] Indeed, it was an addition. Post's portraits of small-town Americans earnestly debating the kind of local issues that would determine their future is a photographic lesson in civics that presages the portraits of democracy in the series Four Freedoms which would propel Norman Rockwell to national attention four years later.

Meanwhile, the topics being debated at town meeting—whether liquor should be sold, the overseeing of the poor, the legality of pinball machines—were all explained in Post's characteristically full captions and reflected the kinds of issues confronting many small towns when the automobile and the radio began both linking people to the larger, outside world and simultaneously threatening their relative innocence. One caption, which reads, "One of the town selectmen voting at a town meeting. The woman who gave him the ballot said, 'If you vote yes for liquor you'd better put your ballot in a box in a different town. We won't let you stay around here long,'" conveys the moral climate that is strongly hinted at in the dour countenances. As compelling as the photographs are, however, Post was exasperated by the reception she received. "The town meeting was somewhat disappointing," she wrote to Stryker, "and I didn't have quite the freedom I'd hoped. There were a couple of old cranks who weren't too pleased about it. I guess it was worth trying anyway."[24] There could not have been too much complaining, however; Post's visit rated no mention at all in the local paper's coverage of Woodstock's town meeting. Then, like Historical Section photographers were bound to do, she moved on, crossing over the Connecticut River into New Hampshire for approximately two weeks before returning to Vermont farther north.[25]

The other significant series is in two parts, illustrating an interesting collision between the timeless rhythms of rural life and the birth of Vermont's ski industry, both occurring on the same farm. First is Clinton Gilbert's farm in winter as a hired hand herds cows through deep snowdrifts and hauls logs by horse (fig. 17), sled, and hand, all activities that portray the unchanging work of countless generations of Vermont farmers. On the same farm, however, is Vermont's first ski tow, which began operating in 1934. In more than a dozen photographs showing children racing down snow-covered slopes, intrepid skiers ascending the hill by rope tow, and skiers warming themselves in the rustic hut Gilbert has constructed, Post has captured the ski industry in Vermont in its infancy. And as if anticipating the state's future, Post wrote in a letter to Stryker that Gilbert "has been really cleaning up on the winter business."[26] Moreover, Post clearly understood the pressures driving economic change in rural places. One caption explains eloquently why Vermonters turned to marketing their hill farms to skiers:

> Skiers come on weekends to Clinton Gilbert's farm. Gilbert has about 150 acres, mainly a dairy farm with 23 cows, and makes about 100 gallons of maple syrup every year. The first ski tow in the United States was built on this farm in 1934 by the White Cupboard Inn, but Gilbert now owns and runs the tow and it has increased his income about 25%. This has enabled him to build a small ski lodge and do many repairs to his property.[27]

Although Post complained years later in an interview that writing captions was her "shortcoming," the evidence suggests otherwise.[28] More than the other Historical Section photographers, who usually wrote short, descriptive captions and, for the most part, let their photographs speak for themselves, Post wrote extensive captions that added another dimension to her photography. A series of photographs she took in Woodstock, for example, depicts a man carrying a bucket through the snow. They could easily be interpreted as all-purpose photographs of a farmer bending to the never-ending work of carrying milk. According to Post's caption, however, the man is a hired hand carrying water to his car's radiator, which he empties every night and refills every morning to avoid the cost of antifreeze. The detail of Post's captions pleased Stryker, who despite his faith in the power of photographs never stopped believing that images were no more than handmaidens to the power of the written word.[29]

In his correspondence with Post during her Vermont tour, Stryker acknowledged that her work in Vermont was noteworthy. "Very good" and "damn good" were some of the compliments he offered in a letter praising her work. One photograph in particular, a scene of downtown Brattleboro taken during a blizzard, he claimed "is going to be an exhibit print and it will be used quite a great deal."[30] However, there were also failures. Apparently, some of Post's Vermont photographs were ruined before they even had a chance to be considered for the file. On 5 March Stryker telegraphed her in Woodstock a second time and told her that her images on 120 film were unusable because they were overlapping.[31]

By the tenth of March, Post had traveled north to Stowe, where, after taking photographs of the village and of houses letting rooms to skiers to show the impact of the fledgling skiing industry, she made her way, on snowshoe or ski, with all her equipment up the snow-covered toll road to the top of Mount Mansfield.[32] At the summit she took panoramic photographs looking in all directions, as well as a series of photographs of skiers relaxing near the forest ranger's rustic hut, which had been built of Mount Mansfield stone as a government project under the Civilian Conservation Corps. According to Post's caption, the ranger, skiing shirtless in the warm spring sunshine, was ferrying supplies up the mountain, but broke his leg on a downhill run shortly after Post took his picture. She also took pictures of skiers resting and eating at the toll-road lodge at the foot of the mountain, and these photographs, perhaps more than any of her other photographs of skiing, capture the

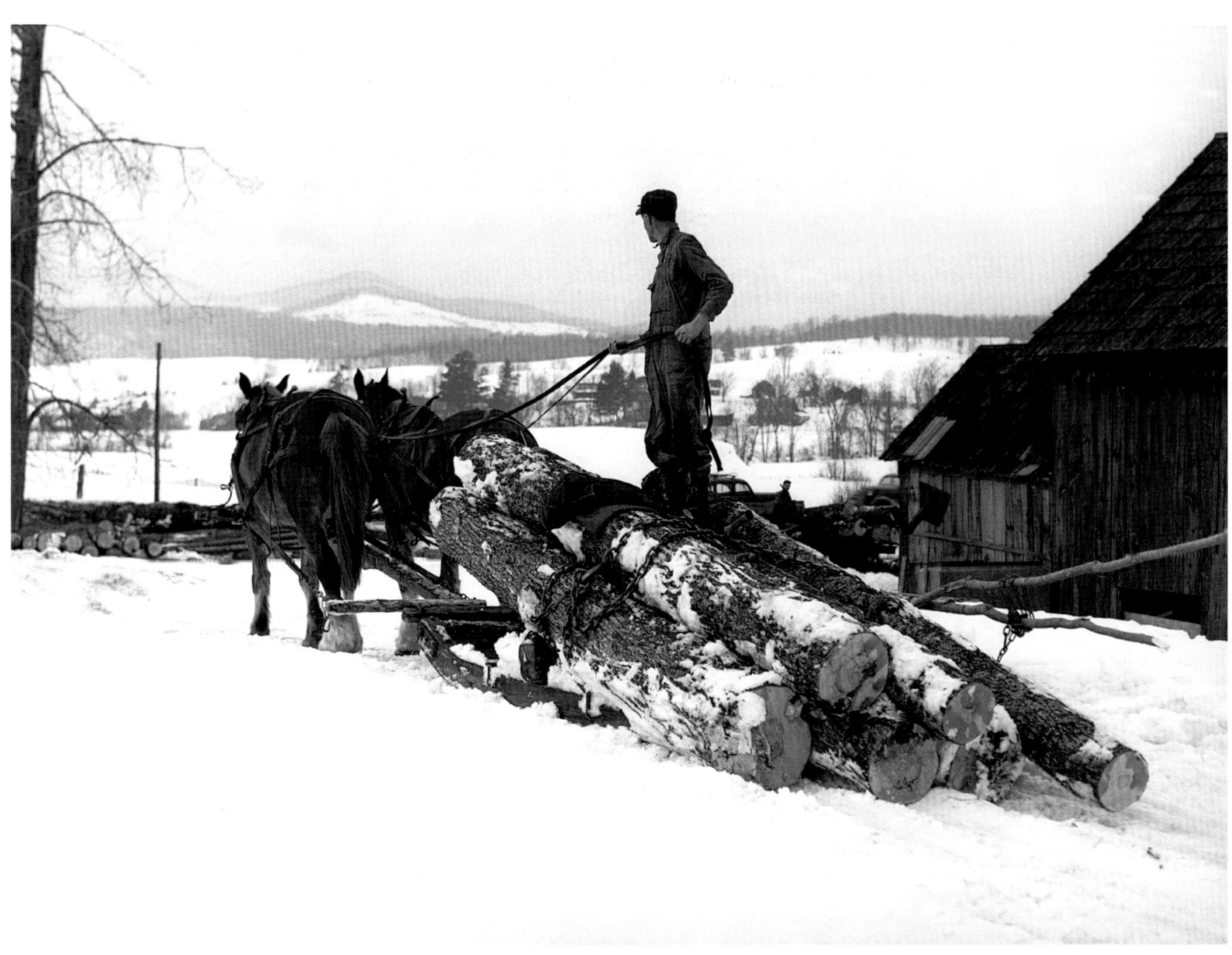

FIGURE 17
Marion Post Wolcott
Waterbury (vicinity), Vt. March 1940. Hired man hauling logs with sled and team on a farm. He said, "There ain't nothing meaner than a log except a women when she wants to be, and they're just as stubborn." They sold the timber to a lumber company.

budding glamour of the sport, particularly as it would blossom in resort towns such as Stowe and Woodstock.

By the middle of March in a year when spring came late, Post was in New Hampshire, which she found disappointing after her Vermont visit. "New Hampshire is a terrible comedown after Vermont," she wrote to Stryker. "It must be even worse in the summer if all these closed cabin 'villages' are full of tourists."[33] New Hampshire was a temporary detour, however. At the end of the month, Post telegrammed Stryker from Vermont, saying "Storm and cold weather subsiding."[34] This was good news for several reasons. Warm weather made her work technically easier, but the photographs she would soon take of dirt roads that had become quagmires suggest that she grew to appreciate the special lessons offered by the time of year Vermonters call mud season. More important, she told Stryker, the change of weather gave her the opportunity to photograph sugaring, but she did not give herself much time. "Returning end of week. Mailing film tomorrow. Letter follows with details," she informed him by telegram.[35]

As she worked her way south Post photographed sugaring in two places in Vermont: Waitsfield and North Bridgewater. She took dozens of photographs in both places, intent on capturing not just the labor and process of sugaring but the cultural environment. Captions written to accompany photographs taken on the four-hundred-acre Frank

Shurtleff farm in North Bridgewater, for example, note that Shurtleff earned $1,000 annually from sugaring, in addition to income earned from lumbering and raising sheep and cows. In referring to the hundred years the Shurtleff farm had been in the family and the thirty-five years that Shurtleff had been sugaring, Post consciously drew attention to the traditions that connect Americans to the land and across time. In her photographs of Shurtleff's hired hand and an attractive young neighbor obviously enjoying themselves as they collect sap and load it onto a horse-drawn sled—as well as in her captions, which refer to sugaring as a "social event"—Post echoes the point made by genre artists, such as Eastman Johnson in *Sugaring Off*, that these time-honored rural traditions are part of the fabric of American community life (fig. 18).

On 27 March Stryker wrote to Russell Lee that Post was "getting some beautiful stuff."[36] Two days later, in another letter to Lee, Stryker wrote, "We have lots of snow pictures, now, for the file. We won't need any more for some time."[37] However, Post had not quite wrapped up her work in Vermont, because on the twenty-ninth, Stryker telegraphed her in Montpelier that "Your pictures have been excellent. Glad you are returning."[38] Unfortunately, if

FIGURE 18
Marion Post Wolcott
North Bridgewater, Vt. April 1940. Frank H. Shurtleff drilling the hole for the spout while tapping a sugar maple tree for gathering sap to make syrup.

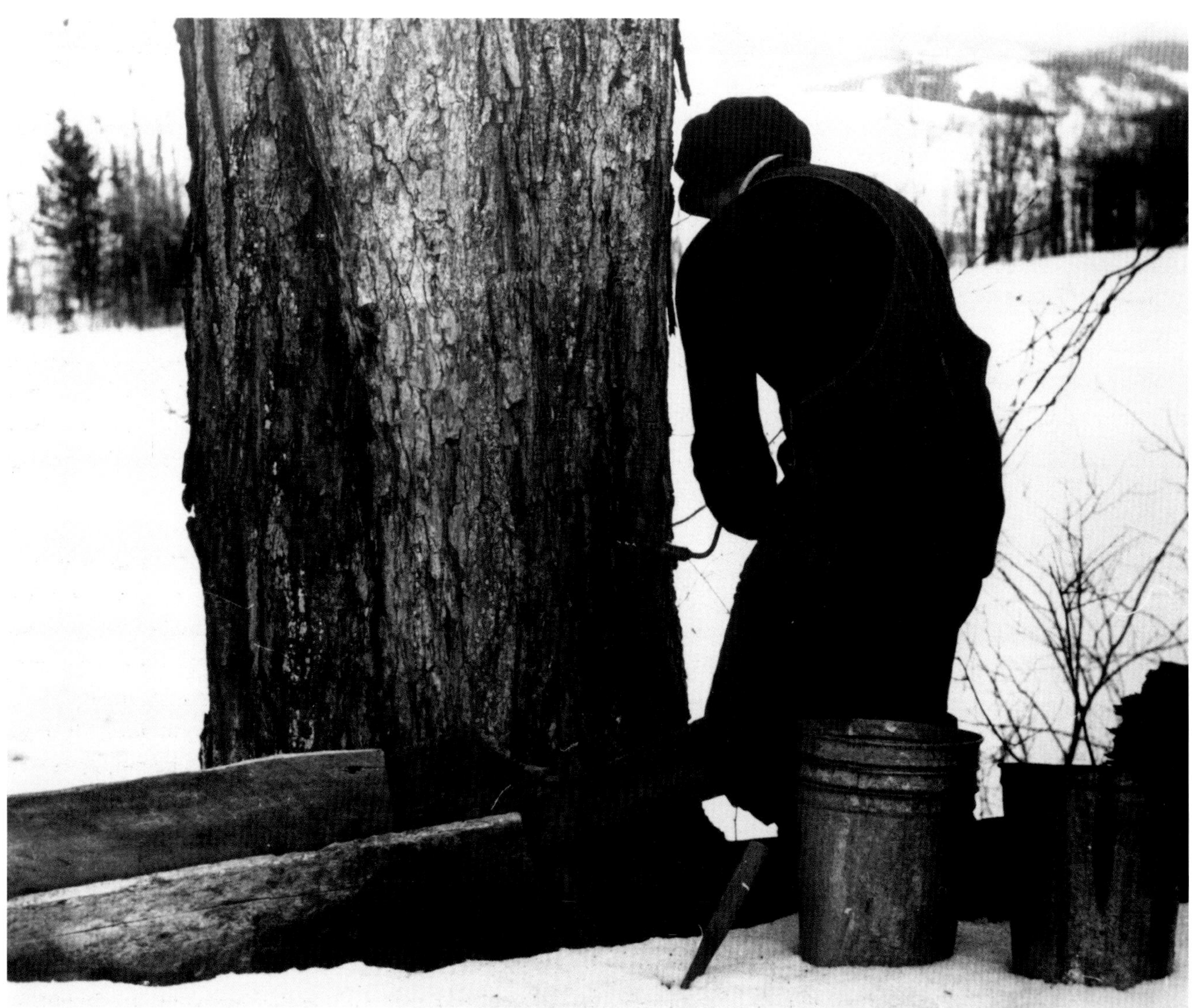

Post took any photographs of the state capital while she was in Montpelier to pick up the telegram, they have not been found.

Back in Washington, Post moved briefly into the apartment she and Rothstein shared on a rotating basis as the other was called out of town on assignment, but the break was short-lived.[39] Almost immediately she was on the road again, this time in the South, where she photographed both the new food stamp program at work and the wealthy enjoying their dances and horse racing. The pictures themselves are innocuous, but when laid beside images of the country's starving laborers, the effect was scathing.[40] She returned to Vermont in March 1941 for a badly needed vacation, dividing her time between Manchester and Stowe for three weeks of skiing. As part of the agreement granting her this long break from fieldwork, she agreed to donate to the file whatever photographs she took, but if she took any, they have not survived among the Vermont images.[41]

Post spent two more years with the section after she took her Vermont photographs. In the spring of 1941 she met and quickly married Lee Wolcott, a widower with two young children who was a high-level bureaucrat in the U.S. Department of Agriculture. Lee Wolcott soon irritated Stryker by demanding that clerks in the Historical Section go back through the tens of thousands of photographs in the file and change his wife's name on every photograph she had taken to reflect her married status. She intended to continue working and for a while accepted road assignments, but by the winter of 1942 she was pregnant. Soon after this discovery, she decided that it was impractical for her to continue work that kept her on the road, away from her husband and two stepchildren. On 20 February 1942 she wired Stryker that she was resigning effective the next day.[42] She returned to her new home in Virginia, embraced motherhood, and essentially retired from professional photography.

Post had a special rapport with the poor she photographed, perhaps because she was willing to perform mundane tasks in her pursuit of a mutually respectful relationship. While on assignment, she was known to care for children, run errands, buy groceries, and peel potatoes, all to help win the trust of FSA clients she wanted to photograph.[43] Many of those she sought to photograph did come to trust her, not just to take their photograph but also to guarantee that it would be used in a dignified way that might help improve their lives. In her experience the middle class proved much more self-conscious and critical of the government's work, and the rich were downright hostile.[44]

Post's winter photographs of Vermont are some of the most beautiful in the Historical Section file. According to shooting-script writer Edwin Rosskam, who was with the Historical Section long enough to see its focus shift from the grim to the more positive, Post "was one of the few photographers who without protest could make pictures that were not necessarily of destitution."[45] Looking back at her Historical Section work thirty years later, Post Wolcott shed more light on this distinction. "I had a different kind of shooting script," she said. "And I had appointments with FSA supervisors to photograph the positive side of the FSA program and work that was being done, and I think I did perhaps more of that than many of the other photographers did."[46] As a result of those evolving directives, Post was able to capture a portrait of Vermont on the eve of monumental changes in the highway system, tourism, and skiing, changes which in many rural towns in Vermont would soon begin to lift the pall of the previous decades.

However, Stryker recognized another distinction between Post and his other photographers. "If you look through the file," he said in an interview in 1963, "you'll find Marion has particularly a great sense of the land, of our terrain, and a feeling of people on the land."[47] In an interview years later Post Wolcott recognized this in herself, too. "I think the landscape and the beauty of it or the vastness of it can tell a great deal about the country and the people." She made no apologies for the beautiful pictures she took. "I did enjoy at that time also photographing the good land, and the lush land, and I thought it had a place in Roy's complete documentation of America."[48] Years later, she recalled her visit to New England in winter, with all its evocative portraits of a frozen land, as one of her favorite assignments.[49]

NOTES

1 / Lange to Stryker, 13 August 1937.

2 / Hurley, *Marion Post Wolcott*, p. 3.

3 / Ibid., p. 15.

4 / Ibid.

5 / Post Wolcott interview, p. 1.

6 / Ibid.

7 / Strand to Stryker, 20 June 1938.

8 / Hurley, *Portrait of a Decade*, p. 108.

9 / Stryker to Post, 14 July 1938.

10 / Hurley, *Marion Post Wolcott*, p. 31.

11 / Ibid.

12 / Post to Stryker, 14 March 1940.

13 / Rosskams interview, p. 13.

14 / Post Wolcott interview, p. 11.

15 / Post to Stryker, 19 February 1940.

16 / Post to Stryker, 24 February 1940.

17 / Post to Stryker, 2 March 1940.

18 / Ibid.

19 / Ibid.

20 / Post to Stryker, 24 February 1940.

21 / Stryker to Post, 27 February 1940.

22 / Stryker to Lee, Rothstein, and Post, 27 February 1940.

23 / Stryker to Post, 4 March 1940.

24 / Post to Stryker, 14 March 1940.

25 / Post to Stryker, 24–25 March 1940.

26 / Post to Stryker, 24 February 1940.

27 / Library of Congress, Prints and Photographs Division, print number LC-USF34-53068-D.

28 / Post Wolcott interview, p. 19.

29 / Stryker and Wood, p. 8.

30 / Stryker to Post, 4 March 1940.

31 / Stryker to Post, 5 March 1940.

32 / Post to Stryker, 9 March 1940.

33 / Post to Stryker, 14 March 1940.

34 / Post to Stryker, 26 March 1940.

35 / Ibid.

36 / Stryker to Lee, 27 March 1940.

37 / Stryker to Lee, 29 March 1940.

38 / Stryker to Post, 29 March 1940.

39 / Hurley, *Marion Post Wolcott*, p. 55.

40 / Ibid., p. 73.

41 / Ibid., p. 105.

42 / Post to Stryker, 20 February 1942.

43 / O'Neal, p. 175.

44 / Post to Stryker, 28–29 July 1950.

45 / Rosskams interview, p. 31.

46 / Post Wolcott interview, p. 9.

47 / Stryker interview, p. 7.

48 / Post Wolcott interview, p. 10.

49 / Ibid., p. 14.

Edwin and Louise Rosskam

The next member of the Historical Section staff to visit Vermont and take photographs may have been Edwin Rosskam. Rosskam, like Edwin Locke in 1937, was not an official photographer for the section. However, according to an interview in 1965, he needed a vacation from his job in Washington organizing publicity for the section and chose to go to Vermont in July 1940.

Rosskam was an American born in Germany who had been imprisoned there as a civilian during World War I because of his dual citizenship. After the war, he immigrated to the United States and spent four years studying at the Pennsylvania Academy of the Fine Arts, in Philadelphia. He exhibited widely as a painter, and then moved to Paris and took up photography. Thereafter he spent several years photographing in Polynesia.

Rosskam takes credit for coining the word "photo-journalism," as he experimented with combining words and photographs while working in Puerto Rico, the South Seas, and the United Sates.[1] His work came to Stryker's attention, and Stryker hired him in early 1938 to provide the kinds of design skills that Ben Shahn had but was too busy to contribute. Officially, Rosskam's title was Editor (Specialist in Visual Information).[2] His job was to cull the ever-growing file for photographs that newspapers, magazines, writers, and book publishers could use, providing not just a reproducible copy of the image but a caption and even a story if it would make the photograph more marketable. Stryker also charged Rosskam with designing and laying out photography exhibits, both large and small, and with preparing shooting scripts.[3] When he was hired, Rosskam agreed to stay for one year. "Now, the understanding between Roy and myself was that I would stay a year, and I stayed one year to the day, and got out of there," Rosskam said years later.[4] However, he did not stay away. As war loomed, he rejoined the section, though he disliked what he called "shuffling photos," and was there when it became the Office of War Information.[5]

Rosskam chafed at working with everyone else's photographs and being denied the chance to take his own. His vacation in Vermont was a welcome opportunity to make a contribution of his own to the file. "I couldn't resist getting a camera once, and once I took a vacation in Vermont," he recalled in 1965. "I said to Roy, 'Could I take some pictures for you? You know, I'll buy my own film and everything.' And he said, 'Oh, here's some film.'"[6] Rosskam also remembered that Stryker took that opportunity to launch into one of his famous monologues:

> He starts rambling about Vermont, and really it didn't sound as if it had anything to do with what you wanted to do at all. You start talking about hills, farmhouses and how people build a little extension on the house for the old people, and about pickled limes, the sky and how to get to Vermont, and who he knew up in Vermont 50 years ago. . . . By the time

you got through listening to him ramble along, you begin to get some sort of formation in your mind of what there was up there.[7]

FIGURE 19
Louise Rosskam
Lincoln (vicinity), Vt. July 1940. Silver salesman who travels from farm to farm trying to sell his wares to farm women.

Unfortunately, if Rosskam took any photographs in Vermont, they do not survive in the section file. However, his effect on the file as a whole was profound, both because he helped direct the kinds of photographs that were taken and because his job included shuffling photographs into the hands of those who would publish and broadcast them. In addition to supplying the images for Anderson's *Home Town*, whose theme influenced the work of at least two photographers in Vermont, Rosskam collaborated on the development of the Face of America series and provided the photographs for three of the books: *San*

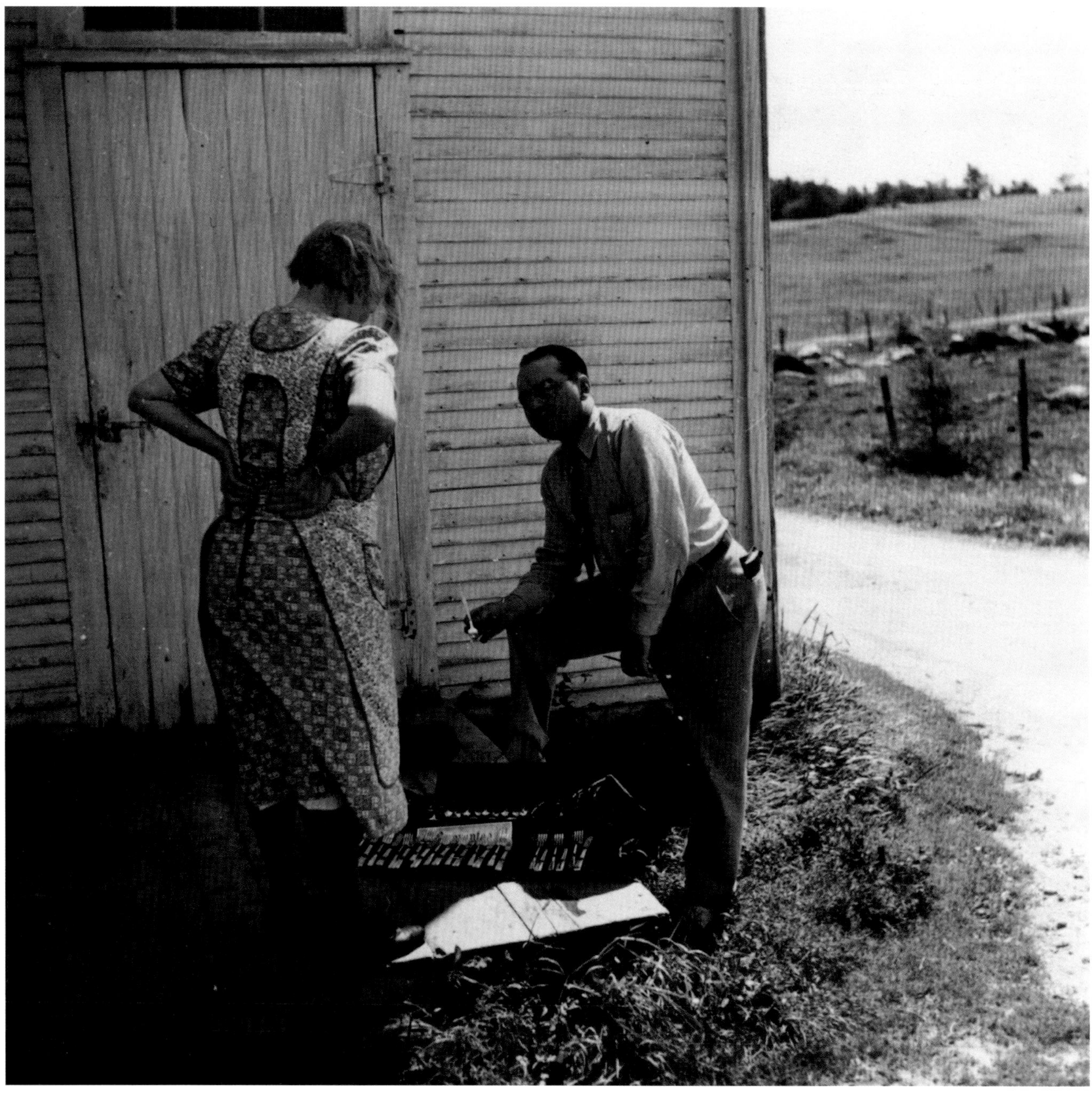

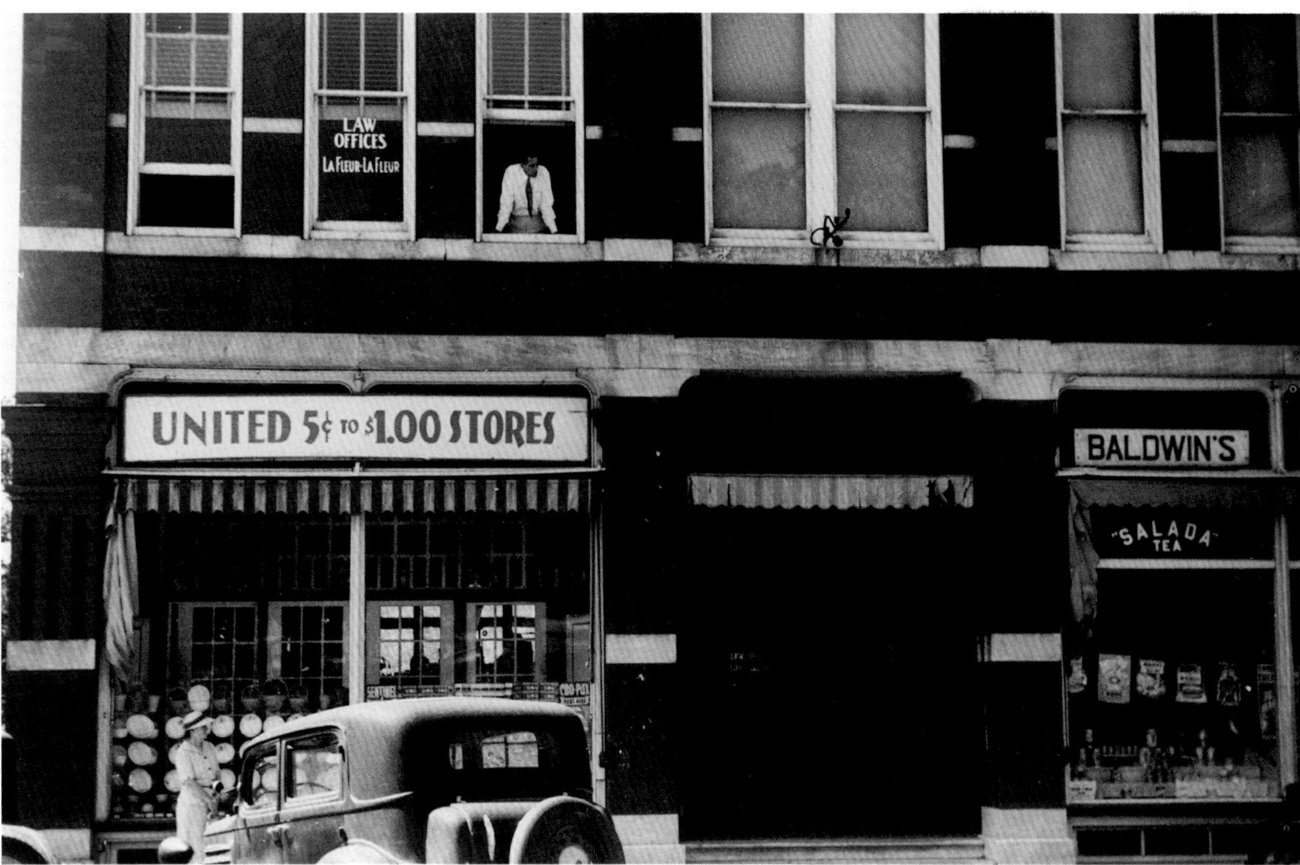

FIGURE 20
Louise Rosskam
Middleburg [Middlebury], Vt. August 1940. Street scene.

Francisco and *Washington Nerve Center*, both published in 1939, and *As Long as the Grass Shall Grow*, published in 1940. He also organized countless exhibitions that brought this aspect of the government's work to the notice of Americans scattered across the country. In that regard, he was instrumental during these years in bringing the Historical Section's work to the public's attention, and in fulfilling the Stryker's mandate to show Americans how Americans lived.

Nowhere is Edwin Rosskam's influence more apparent than in the work of his wife, Louise, who also visited Vermont in the summer of 1940. A photographer, like her husband, but with less experience, Louise Rosskam was working not for the Historical Section but for *American Magazine* in Washington when someone she knew suggested a city-country exchange and directed her to a relative's farm in Lincoln, Vermont. Louise Rosskam took the train north, traveling alone, and spent two months on the farm of Milo and Magdalene Lathrop. Milo Lathrop, a 1926 graduate of Middlebury College who had spent 1936–1937 working for the Vermont Resettlement Administration, was farming at the time on a family homestead and working as a field representative and educational director for a variety of labor organizations in the state. Louise Rosskam was not on assignment for the Historical Section and she lacked a car, making her dependent on the excursions of others to find changes of scene, but her photographs show that she was a sensitive chronicler of rural domestic life in and around Addison County. Her images include a door-to-door silver salesman exhibiting his wares (fig. 19), a farm wife canning beans, the interiors of farm houses, and a woman washing clothes in her motor-driven washing machine on the back porch of her farm house. She also took several poignant photographs of small-town life, including pictures of a band concert and a church raffle in Lincoln, a businessman observing a lazy street scene in Middlebury (fig. 20), and an elderly couple setting up a popcorn roaster on the green in front of the town hall in Bristol. Her images of farming are unlike Rothstein's pictures of farming, in which a photograph of a man scything is really a visual metaphor for hard work; rather, hers are true portraits of the farmers themselves, each posed in his field or standing beside his produce. In Addison she captured a church and a Grange hall standing side by side and almost indistinguishable in their architecture—an ironic statement about the importance of these two institutions to small-town life.

After Louise Rosskam became familiar with Lincoln, she undertook something that no official Historical Section photographer attempted in Vermont: she went aloft. Begging a ride to the airport in Bristol, where a grass runway and a hangar holding four planes constituted one of the twelve airports then in Vermont, she asked for a flying lesson.[8] For fifteen dollars, she was given a plane and an instructor, but before they took off, she admitted that her true purpose was to take photographs. The crew at the airport was obliging. First they strapped her in tightly so she could lean out the window and take photographs, but when it became apparent that her Roloflex camera would not permit her to lean out the window far enough to shoot straight down, they removed the door to further accommodate her needs.[9] Her aerial shots—fewer than half a dozen, and primarily of the Lathrop farm in Lincoln—are unique among the Historical Section photographs in Vermont both for their perspective and for conveying a panoramic sense of the state's land-use patterns (fig. 21).

In an interview in the autumn of 2000, Louise Rosskam explained that her photographs found their way into the Historical Section file along a typical path. "The first thing all the photographers asked Roy when they returned to the office was, 'Do you want to see the pictures?'" she recalled. "He looked at mine and said, 'Oh, we'll keep these for the file.'" For the next sixty years, however, Louise Rosskam's husband, Edwin, was credited with the photographs she took in and around Addison County during her cultural exchange. Only very recently did she reclaim them as her own.[10]

NOTES

1 / Rosskams interview, p. 2.

2 / Ibid., p. 1.

3 / Stryker to Edwin Rosskam, 13 July 1939.

4 / Rosskams interview, p. 1.

5 / Ibid., p. 4.

6 / Ibid., p. 35.

7 / Ibid.

8 / Crane, *Let Me Show You Vermont*, p. 311.

9 / Louise Rosskam interview, 15 October 2000.

10 / Louise Rosskam interview, 10 November 2000.

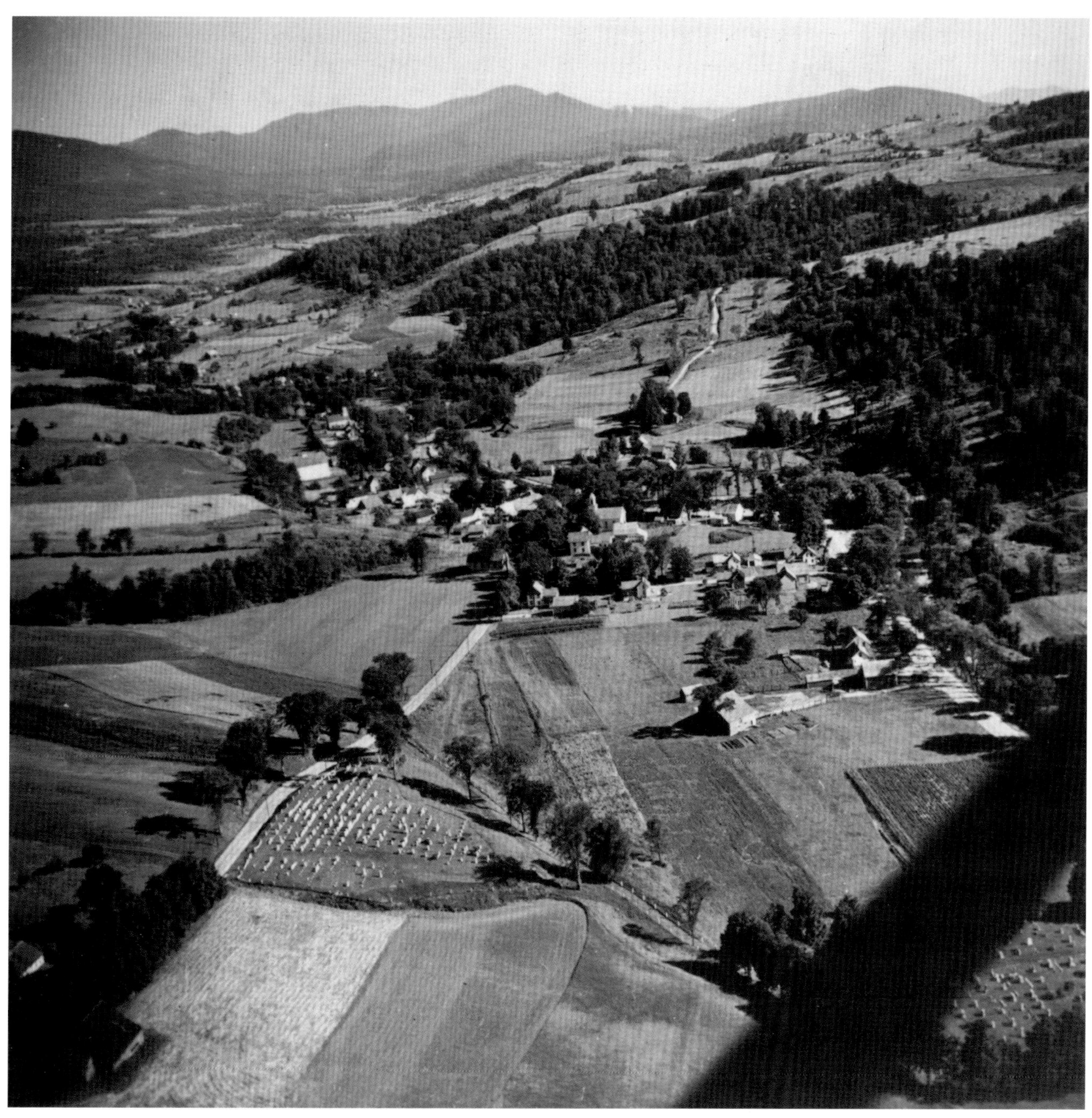

FIGURE 21

Louise Rosskam

Lincoln, Vt. July 1940. Air view of a cemetery and town.

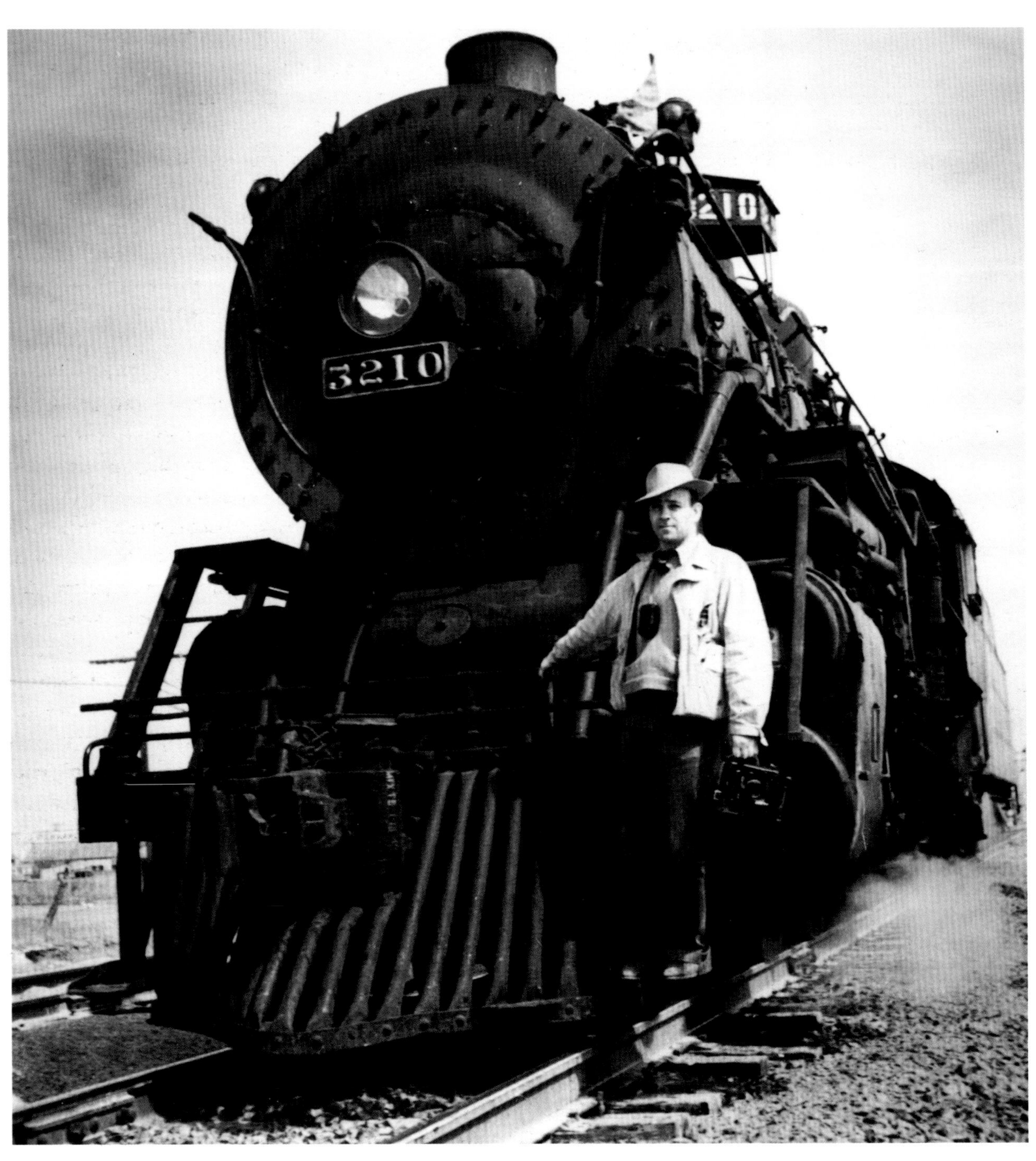
3210

Jack Delano

FIGURE 22 (opposite)
Jack Delano, Farm Security Administration/Office of War Information photographer, full-length portrait, holding camera, standing on front of locomotive, c. 1943.

More than fifty years after Jack Delano's last professional visit to Vermont, an element of confusion still exists regarding whether he visited the state on his first Historical Section assignment in New England (fig. 22). Hired by Roy Stryker in May 1940, Delano went out on assignment to southern Virginia before being sent north in the late summer to take photographs in the northeastern states. Stryker was probably not in the office when Delano left. A letter from Russell Lee to Stryker indicates that the director of the division was in Vermont vacationing at his cottage on Lake Eden in early August.[1] Nevertheless, Delano had a nine-page script, titled "Information on New England," that focused on agriculture and New England's preparation for war. He also had instructions to read Van Wycks Brooks's *The Flowering of New England,* a celebration of the region's values and rich literary history that went through seventeen printings in 1936, the year it was first published. The 8 × 10 camera he was given was the one used by Walker Evans.[2]

Delano and his wife, Irene, who was his assistant and traveling companion, were on the road throughout New England for almost six months. He fell in love with the three-way, convertible-lens camera, using it to take photographs of landscapes and architecture in the New England towns he passed through.[3] To document war preparedness, he took photographs of textile mills, iron foundries, machine shops, and fishing boats. He also devoted a significant part of the assignment to photographing migrant farm workers on the last leg of their migration northward from Florida, along the coast, to the potato fields of Aroostock County, Maine.[4] Sometime during the early days of autumn, Stryker wrote to Delano and asked him to keep an eye out for autumn pictures, which he said were in demand: "These should be rather the symbol of autumn . . . cornfields, pumpkins. . . . Emphasize the idea of abundance—the 'horn of plenty'—and pour maple syrup over it—you know, mix well with white clouds and put on a sky-blue platter." Stryker had ulterior motives in issuing this directive, however. As much as he wanted to add pretty pictures to the ever-growing file, he wanted to provide the government with photographs to use in an intensifying propaganda war with Hitler. "I know your damned photographer's soul writhes, but to hell with it," he continued, making no apologies for the saccharin assignment and mixing bluster with seriousness. "Do you think I give a damn about a photographer's soul with Hitler at our doorstep? You are nothing but camera fodder to me."[5]

In an interview done years after the Historical Section office closed, Irene Delano recalled that this swing through New England in the fall of 1940 and early winter of 1941 "was just a fantastic trip, and we were in every state."[6] However, if it is true that the Delanos visited every New England state in 1940, then either Delano did not take any photographs in Vermont or none survive. It seems more likely that they missed Vermont, hugging the coast instead up through Connecticut, Rhode Island, Massachusetts, New Hampshire, and Maine, dogging the heels of the migrant farm workers and uncovering preparations for war in the industrial belt between Connecticut and New Hampshire. In all probability, another year passed before Delano brought his camera to Vermont.

Jack Delano was born Jacob Ovcharov on 1 August 1914 in the Ukraine, in a small town obliterated by the Nazis during World War II. The Ovcharovs immigrated to the United Sates in 1923, arriving in New York City on the Fourth of July, and stayed at first with relatives just outside of Philadelphia.[7] Ovcharov's mother was a dentist, and his father was a mathematician forced into furniture making by the dislocation. Nevertheless, the family home was a cultural center for music, literature, and art, and Ovcharov and his brother were both steered into the arts at an early age. After graduating from high school, Ovcharov won a partial scholarship to the Pennsylvania Academy of the Fine Arts, where he studied to become an illustrator and met Irene, his future wife and the sixteen-year-old cousin of the painter Ben Shahn.[8]

Art school educated Ovcharov in ways he had not expected: "[The 1930s] was a time for social awareness and political involvement. The New Deal government had raised the consciousness of people toward the complex problems facing the country, and newspaper headlines made us aware of the threat of war."[9] Among the activities he pursued outside the classroom, Ovcharov painted murals for African American conventions and picket signs for the stevedores' union strike. He also worked on films that promoted boycotts of Japanese products.

In 1935 Ovcharov won a traveling scholarship from the Pennsylvania Academy of the Fine Arts to go to Europe. In his search for what he called the art of "ordinary people"—simple, hardworking people like his parents—he traveled to Paris, England, Italy, Austria, Holland, and Spain to study paintings that captured the dignity of plain people. However, his education once again took unexpected turns. After he encountered cubism, abstract expressionism, and surrealism, the traditional approach to painting taught at the Pennsylvania academy felt stifling. Moreover, he was growing increasingly intrigued by a camera he had purchased to try to capture ordinary people on film.[10]

Back in the United States, Ovcharov changed his name to Jack Delano. Delano was the surname of a friend, and Jack was borrowed from the pugilist Jack Dempsey. He took a job with the Federal Arts Project, one of President Franklin D. Roosevelt's federal employment programs.[11] Working as a photographer for the Index of American Design, he quickly grew restless because he found the work unfulfilling. Later in his life he wrote:

> I was interested in social conditions and I thought the camera could be a means of communicating how I felt about problems facing the country and that therefore I could perhaps influence the course of events. I thought I could portray ordinary working people in photographs with the same compassion and understanding that Van Gogh had shown for the peasants of Holland with pencil and paintbrush.[12]

Determined to find work that was more satisfying, Delano convinced the Federal Arts Project to sponsor him for one month while he lived with and photographed a mining family in Pottsville, Pennsylvania, in the heart of the state's illegal mining activity. The photographs of desperate living and working conditions that he took over the course of that month were exhibited and caught the attention of Paul Strand, whose work Delano had long admired. Delano particularly appreciated what he called Strand's "respect for the thing in front of him." Looking back years later at Strand's influence on his work, Delano wrote, "the thing in front of me became the basic reason for taking a photograph."[13]

Trying to launch a career in New York, Delano became aware of Historical Section photographs being published in magazines such as *Look*, *Survey Graphic*, and *Saturday Review* and in Dorothea Lange's *American Exodus* and Walker Evans's *American Photographs.*[14] "When I saw the first FSA photographs," Delano said years later in an interview, "this was a dream come true. Here was Washington, the government, the Federal government, actually doing this kind of thing which I had been struggling to do myself here in Schuykill County [Pennsylvania]."[15] Hoping to join this august company, he sent copies of his mining work to Roy Stryker, who wrote back, "Sorry. No openings available. Good work. Do not give up hope. Read the following books," and there followed a long list of books on "economics, geography, history, sociology, and even a government pamphlet on canning vegetables."[16] In need of work, Delano returned to New York City and took a job with the United Fund, replacing photographer Lewis Hine, whose arrangement with the Fund had broken down and who, like Delano, had tried unsuccessfully to get work with the Farm Security Administration Historical Section.[17] Several months later, when Arthur Rothstein was poised to leave the section, Stryker hired Delano to take his place for the standard $2,300 per year plus mileage and a per diem, starting on 6 May 1940. Stryker also ordered his new employee to read an edition of Russell Smith's *North America.*[18] Virtually overnight Delano had to get a driver's license, learn to drive, and buy a car. Like the other Historical Section photographers before him, he was about to begin a life on the road.

It was typical of the experience of new photographers in the Historical Section that Delano began his new job anticipating working with some of the photographic giants of the day. Among the corps of distinguished photographers at the section whom Delano was especially keen to meet were Ben Shahn and Walker Evans, people, he later said, "whose work I admired very much." In time, he did meet and develop a warm friendship with Ben Shahn, but the working arrangements of the Historical Section, he said, were such that, "I never met any of them. Everybody was, as usual, in parts of the country, everybody was always out and you never saw anybody except by pure chance."[19]

Like other Historical Section photographers who developed routines to adapt to the long road trips they endured, Delano evolved his own methods for surviving on the road. From the beginning, Irene, his wife, accompanied him everywhere, just as Paul Taylor accompanied his wife, Dorothea Lange, when his schedule permitted, even though the practice was officially prohibited. Stryker looked the other way, perhaps because Irene was an able assistant. Early on she kept a log of the light, exposure, and focus of every photograph Delano took, so they could better analyze the prints when they saw them.[20] Over time, that system was abandoned, but she remained at his side as long as Delano was with the Historical Section, jotting down information for captions and helping to break the ice in the never-ending parade of new situations they encountered.

Unlike some of the other Historical Section photographers, such as Dorothea Lange and Walker Evans, who regarded their photographs as singular works of art, and who, therefore, tried to maintain complete control over their work by developing the day's images in cold water bathrooms on the road, Delano appreciated Stryker's conviction that the section's photographs were meant for the masses. He trusted the technicians in Washington to produce photographs that were what he called "technically good" for "reproduction and for mass distribution."[21] He said in an interview, "This seemed like heaven to have some very good equipment and some experts who knew how to process and develop your films, that you could just turn over to and not have to worry about it."[22] Once a week when he was on the road, he would visit a post office and pick up the previous week's work, which included contact prints of all the larger negatives and 5 × 7 enlargements of his 35mm work. He and Irene edited together, choosing those they would reject by writing "kill" across the face and halfway tearing the 5 × 7 prints they did not like. Afterward, they spent hours writing captions for the photographs that survived this field review.[23] This arrangement sometimes meant, however, that technical errors gave rise to small crises. Stryker telegraphed Delano, for example, that his shutter speed was too slow to capture the Rutland fair's sulky races, but by the time the telegram was delivered, the fair had ended.[24]

No other Historical Section photographer covered Vermont as extensively as Delano did from midsummer to midautumn 1941. Although he spent only a little more time in Vermont than Arthur Rothstein did in the autumn of 1937, Delano took photographs in at least fifty-one different locations, compared to the twenty-four locations that Rothstein photographed. Indeed, Delano's restless sweep of the state suggests that he rarely spent two nights in a row in the same bed during his stay in Vermont.

The trip apparently included a visit with the Strykers at Eden Mills; in a letter to his boss Delano refers to the enjoyable time he and Irene spent with them "at the Garden of Eden Mills."[25] The northernmost Vermont photograph was taken in East Berkshire along a meandering line of photographed sites that begins in Lowell—by now familiar territory to Historical Section photographers—and ends in Sheldon Springs. The southernmost photograph was taken in Vernon, where Route 5 enters southeastern Vermont from Massachusetts. In between, according to a hand-drawn map of his travels he sent to Stryker, Delano worked his way along a big loop from Rutland to Burlington to the Northeast Kingdom, and then back through Rutland to Bennington.[26] State and country fairs often determined his route. In early August, for example, he left Springfield for Rutland, and then went on to Burlington. Afterward he went to Enosburg Falls, then south in early September to the state fair in Rutland, north again to Essex for the Champlain Valley Exposition, and then south again to the fair in Tunbridge.[27]

In a letter Delano wrote to Stryker in early August, shortly after his arrival in Vermont, the photographer reflects on what he has found and how it has affected him. "I'm just about to leave Springfield after completing what might be called the first phase of my attack on Vermont," he informs his boss.

> I have looked around, I have talked to people, and have been very much impressed by the Vermont hills. Most of the work I've done so far has been on what the land looks like and what the towns are like. I'm really very fond of the hills and valleys here so there are quite a lot of shots of long distance views of hill farms, of rolling fields, of little towns away down in the valley and checkerboards of woods and fields on a mountainside—some of the shots will no doubt drip with "Pure Vermont Maple Syrup" but that [is] all right.[28]

It would appear that no FSA photographer enjoyed Vermont more than Delano did. He brought to his work in the state a sense of humor and a sharp, sensitive eye for the incongruous, the ironic, and the absurd. More obviously than Arthur Rothstein, for example, he composed his photographs and placed many of his subjects in a rich context. While Marion Post excelled at portraying the "good earth," and Russell Lee was unmatched in evoking the physical and spiritual destitution of poverty, no one was better than Delano in capturing the tender moment.

All this is evident in the photographs he took from late August to late September at a small American Legion fair in Bellows Falls, at the Champlain Valley Exposition in Essex Junction, at the Vermont State Fair in Rutland, and at the Tunbridge World's Fair (fig. 23). These pictures are full of life and energy: Ferris wheels and merry-go-rounds are frozen in split-second time; barkers hawk sideshows such as the singing talents of the "Fattest Family in the World" (fig. 24) and the wonders of "Charlie Chaplin Chickens"; clouds of dust rise from the racetracks as horses thunder by; the exuberant feet of square and folk dancers are forever poised above dance floors; and fairgoers enthusiastically try their hands at all sorts of games. However, there are other sides to all this action. Photographs of a couple looking at the "Vagabond," a shining new travel trailer, and at a Maytag exhibit featuring the latest in washing machines, show not just the future of technology but a generation's hopes. Couples photographed from the rear with their arms entwined, and men captured from the same angle with liquor bottles protruding from their pants pockets convey more than their faces ever could about their reasons for coming to the fair, just as a

FIGURE 23
Jack Delano
Tunbridge, Vt. September 1941. The parade at the World's Fair.

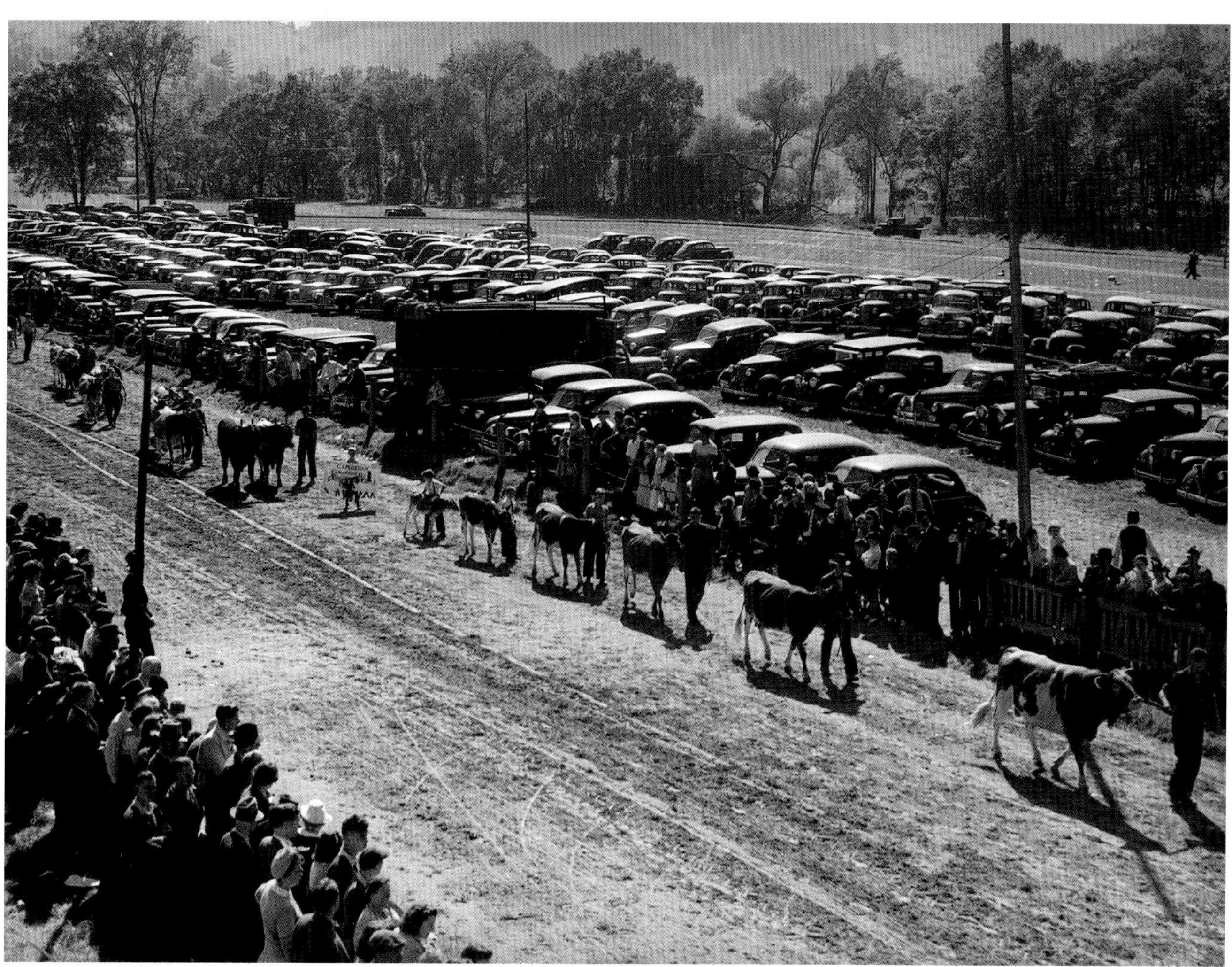

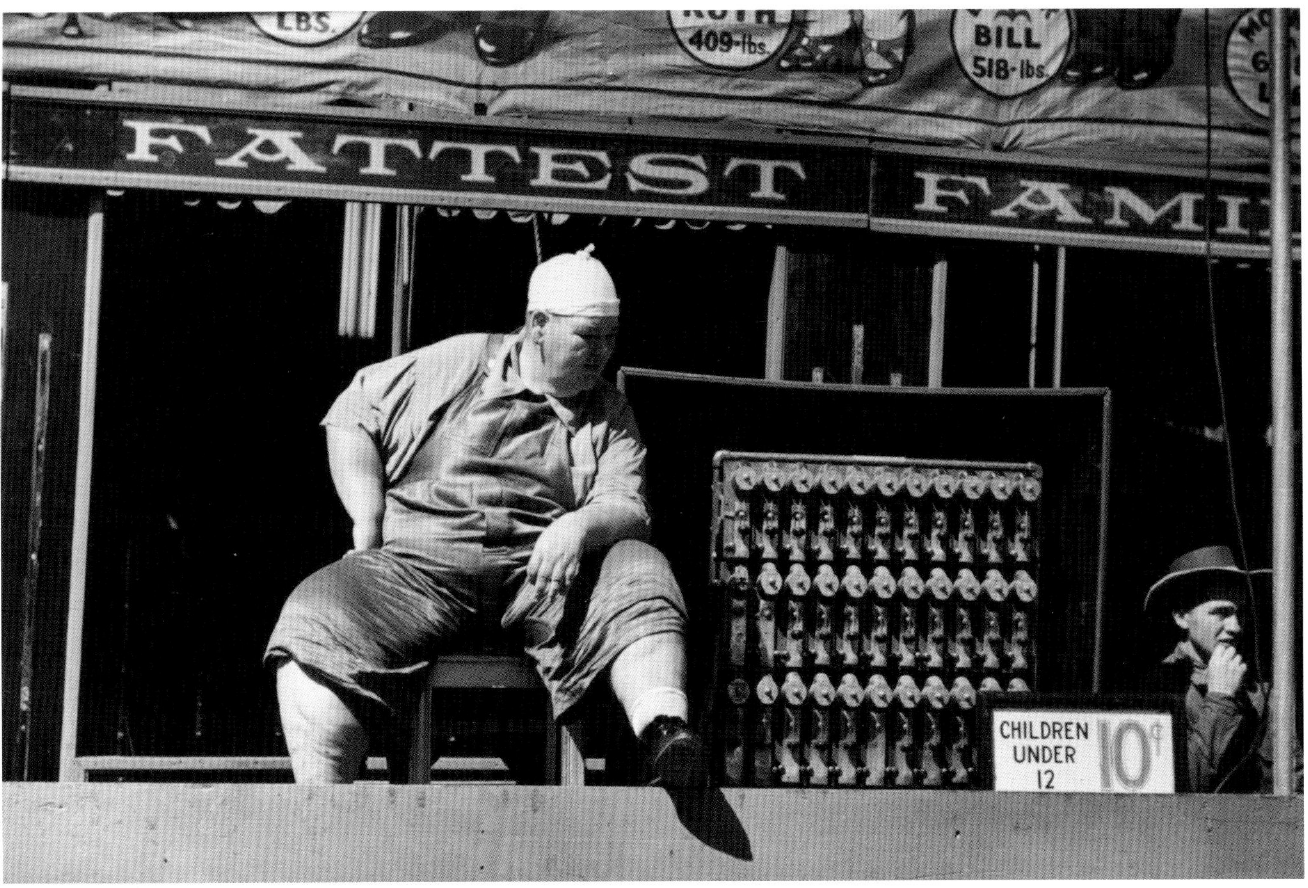

FIGURE 24
Jack Delano
Rutland, Vt. September 1941. A side show at the Vermont State Fair.

touching picture of a well-dressed elderly couple asleep on a blanket beside their car speaks volumes about their relationship. One of Delano's funniest photographs captures an elderly couple at the Vermont State Fair looking exhausted and dour and resting beside a sign that says "mirth" (fig. 25).

To accomplish all this, Delano approached his assignments methodically and meticulously. In an interview Delano confessed that as a person reared in a city, he had no idea what to expect from country fairs when he was asked to photograph them. He and his wife developed the habit, therefore, of scouting the fairs for a day without his camera in hand and developing their own shooting scripts. What eventually comprised the script, he said, "would be the most detailed and, for us, exciting things that we could imagine," including people, what they wore, how they looked, and what kind of tobacco they chewed.[29] Keeping signs in mind he even included non-visual subjects such as language and accents, which seem unusual until one remembers that Stryker was fond of urging his photographers to try to capture on film subjects such as the taste of maple syrup and the quiet of a summer day.

The fairs also presented Delano with a unique opportunity. During the years when the Historical Section photographers were in the field, Kodachrome, invented in 1935, was still an experimental film whose uses and possibilities were only beginning to be recognized. Of all the section photographers, only Delano used color film in Vermont, and of the photographs he took, only a handful made it into the file. Apparently the problem was not just with the photographers' inexperience with the new kind of film. In a letter to Stryker,

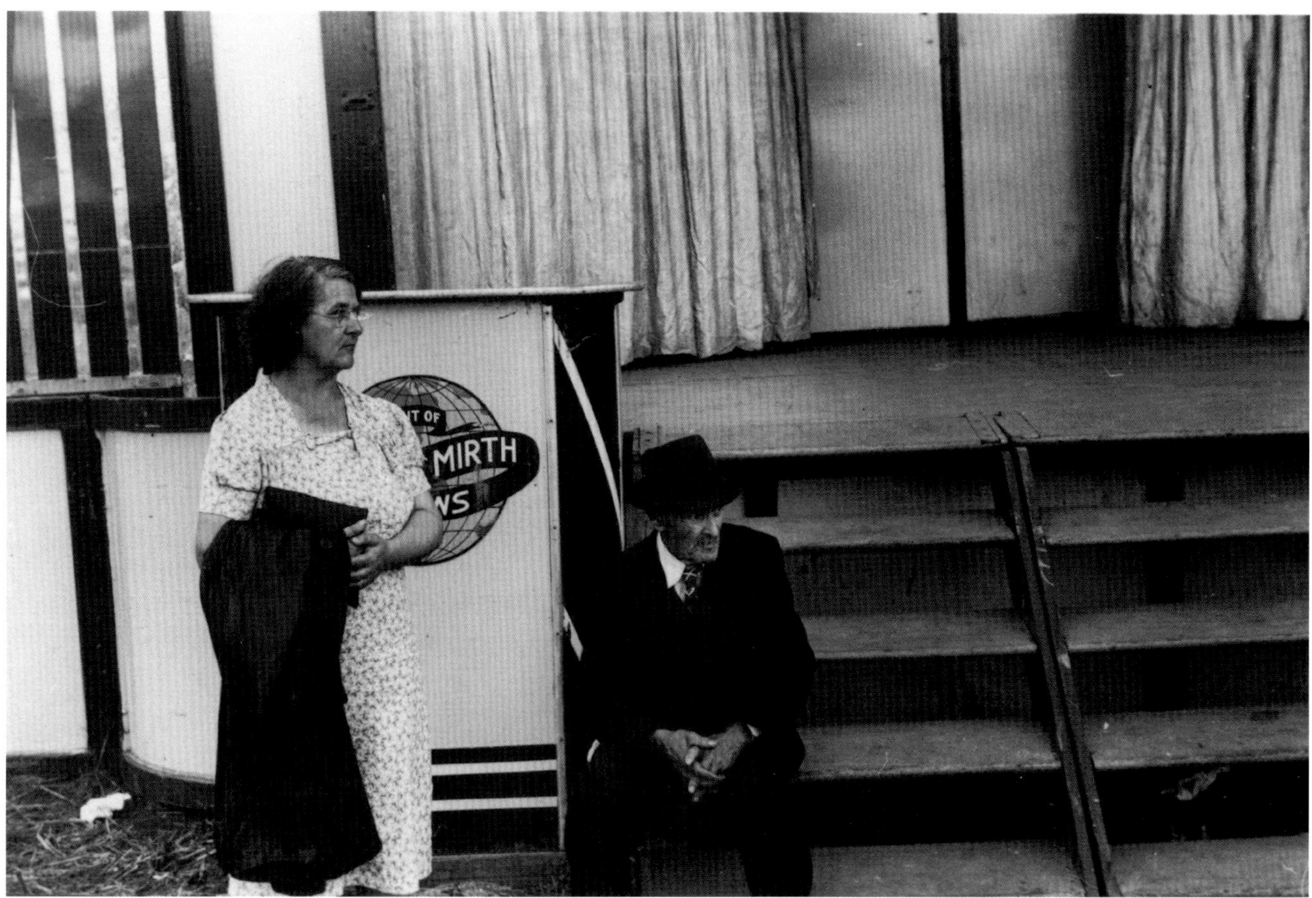

FIGURE 25
Jack Delano
Tired visitors at the Vermont State Fair, Rutland, September 1941.

Delano alluded at length to problems in placing the photographs once they were printed. Many publications were simply unable to reproduce them. Moreover, color prints could not be sent out the way black-and-white prints were; rather, the film itself had to be sent, and no one, especially Stryker, was comfortable giving up control of the film to outsiders. Delano suggested contacting "outlets" before assignments were undertaken so use of the color could be agreed upon and assured.[30]

Nevertheless, he was undeterred by the challenges presented by this innovation. "You know how often we see color in our travels used in an astonishing way," he wrote to Stryker. "If Kodachrome can do the job I'd like to do a series of these things in which the local color is the important thing."[31] Apparently he had been inspired by shooting a roll of Kodachrome at the Rutland fair two weeks earlier (fig. 26). "The place was so full of dazzling color," he had written to his boss after he finished up at the fair, "that I'd like to shoot several rolls of Kodachrome at the Tunbridge Fair next week. Maybe I can get a fairly complete story of the fair in color."[32] Unfortunately, the color film did not arrive in time for the Tunbridge World's Fair, and he was forced to return to strictly black and white. However, he did promise Stryker that he would try to get up to Eden Mills to take a Kodachrome photograph of Belvidere Mountain from Lake Eden.[33] If such a photograph exists, it may have been a gift to the Strykers; nothing like it survives in the file.

Arriving in Vermont relatively late in the Historical Section's existence, Delano faced not only the challenge of photographing fresh subjects that differed from those captured by earlier photographers but also complications arising from the growing popularity of

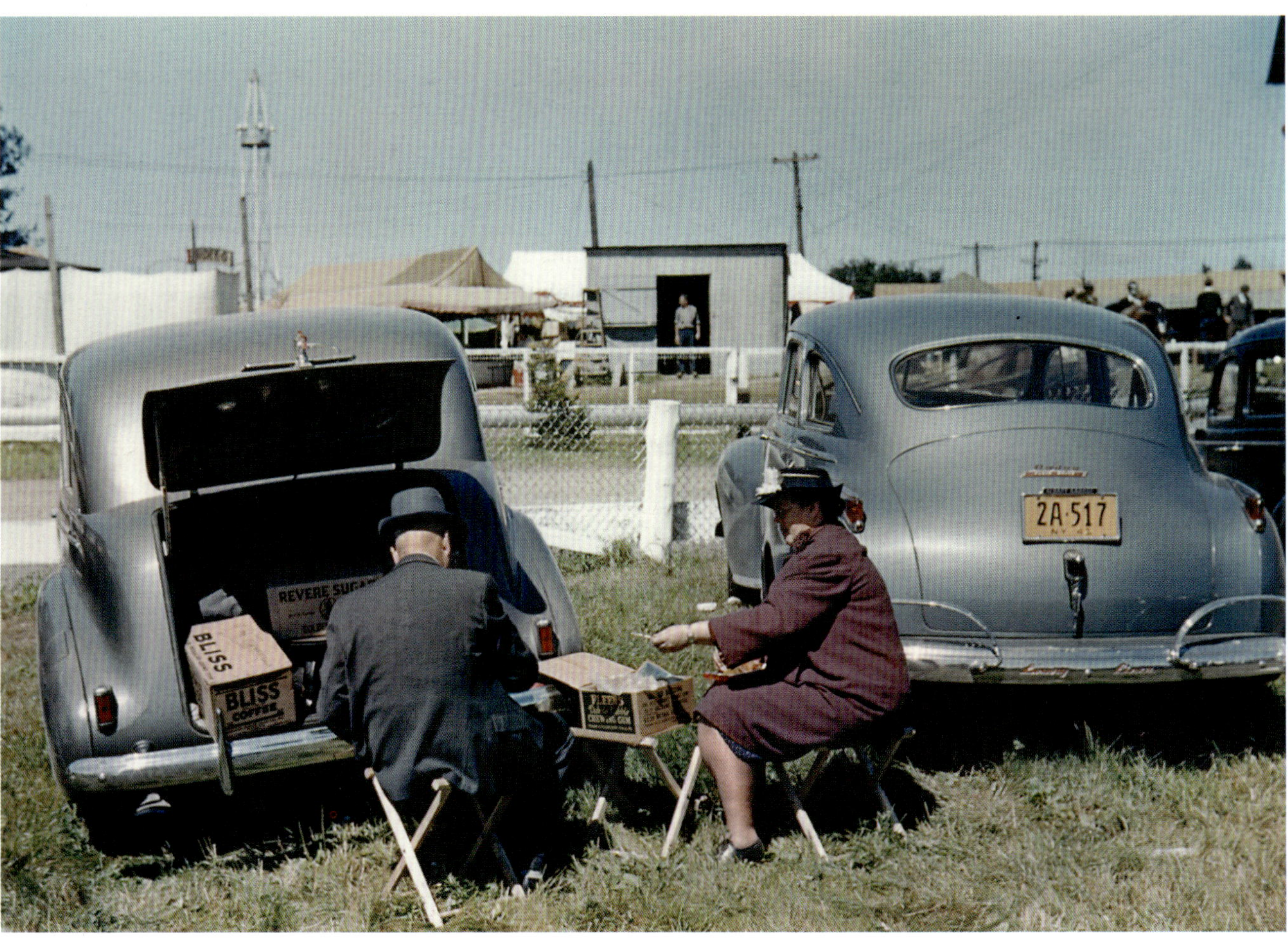

FIGURE 26

Jack Delano

At the Vermont State Fair, Rutland, September 1941.

Collection of the Richard F. Brush Art Gallery, St. Lawrence University. Gift of Rick Jeffrey (parent of Richard Jeffrey, Jr., '85).

documentary photography in general. For example, in trying to photograph the Tunbridge World's Fair, Delano initially met resistance from fairgoers that bewildered him. Finally someone told him that *Yankee* magazine had already sent someone to cover the fair and that *Life* magazine a week earlier had sent both a writer and a photographer, whose style of ordering around fairgoers had irritated people and disillusioned them about becoming icons for the good country life.[34] Consequently, the Delanos were compelled to wander the fair for several days without their cameras until they had earned back the trust of people who would once again allow themselves to be photographed.[35]

More than those from the Historical Section who had preceded him, Delano traveled around Vermont photographing FSA clients. His assignment took him to twelve FSA farms in ten towns, including the Eliot Miller farm in Castleton, the Horatio Weaver farm in Tinmouth, the Edward Grant farm near East Alburg, the Silas Butson farm in Athens, the Ray Lyman farm near Castleton, and the rented farm of Isadore Lavictoire near Rutland.[36] As was the case at least half the time with the Historical Section's photographs, some of the farmers and a number of other subjects were not specifically named in the official captions released to the press, even though the photographers often supplied specific names, as Delano did in this case, for the unofficial caption sheet that would remain buried in the file in Washington. Although Stryker desperately wanted to photograph the faces of struggling Americans to personalize their plight, the omission, in general, of so many names from the captions suggests both that the Historical Section was sensitive to the dignity of the FSA clients, who might have been embarrassed to have their difficult circumstances broadcast to a curious nation, and that Stryker felt there was a certain value in stressing humanity over individuality. Certainly, every FSA client's case was unique, but the problem the populist Stryker wanted to address was less about individuals than it was about the inequities of class structure.

No more than a handful of photographs survive in the file from any of the farms, with one exception, the William Gaynor farm in Fairfield, which Delano clearly identified on each photograph. The Historical Section file contains more than sixty photographs of the Gaynor farm, located halfway between Burlington and the Canadian border, making it one of the most photographed subjects in Vermont's FSA history. When Delano visited their farm in 1941, William Gaynor was thirty-five, his wife, Elizabeth, two years older, and together they had five children, ranging in age from almost two to nine. According to Delano's extended notes, the Gaynors had lived on the 150-acre farm for four years, the first year as tenants, the last three as owners. The family milked twenty-five cows and sent the milk to the nearby Hood creamery. However, according to town land records, the size of the farm was closer to 135 acres, and William and Elizabeth had bought it only two years earlier, in July, from William Gaynor's parents, who owned a four-hundred-acre farm elsewhere in town. Delano's notes also reveal that William and Elizabeth Gaynor were without a car and therefore dependent on a grocer's truck that visited the farm once a week to supply their food. They admitted to being isolated, confessing to Delano that they had not traveled the thirty miles to St. Albans, the nearest small city, in two years.[37] Although Delano's photographs are memorable, the farm apparently did not provide the kind of living the Gaynors had hoped for. Despite government assistance from the FSA, the quiet desperation of their lives drove them to sell their farm in 1948 and move to western Massachusetts in search of better paying work. Two years later, the senior Gaynors also left farming, having lost their farm in a bankruptcy settlement.

The Gaynor photographs illustrate once again Stryker's fascination with process and with photographing a topic from a variety of angles in order to capture it in its entirety. Never one to believe that any single photograph in the file, no matter how evocative, fulfilled the FSA mission to document the American scene, Stryker insisted to the end, particularly in light of the ever-growing richness of the Historical Section file, that the file itself was a document that could only be appreciated in its entirety. The Gaynor photographs reinforce Stryker's idea that depth and breadth of coverage would give dimension to the collection. They show William Gaynor performing the tasks of farming, juxtaposing modern milking machines with horse-drawn plows (fig. 27); Elizabeth Gaynor preparing dinner, washing her children's faces, and canning tomatoes; and the Gaynor children walking to school, working in the fields, and romping on their way to bed. Delano captures in the grand picture and the small details the scope and relentlessness of farm work: its never-ending physical demands, its often meager returns, the way it draws a family together in pursuit of a common goal, and the way it circumscribes the horizons of people who are chained to it.

The Gaynor photographs are also part of Delano's larger goal. Writing to Stryker in early September, Delano bragged that he could spout milk prices, butterfat requirements for different markets, and hay yields per acre, all because he "had come to appreciate what an important industry milk is and what the milk check means to every family up here." He determined to photograph what he called "the problem of milk" by tracking the process of

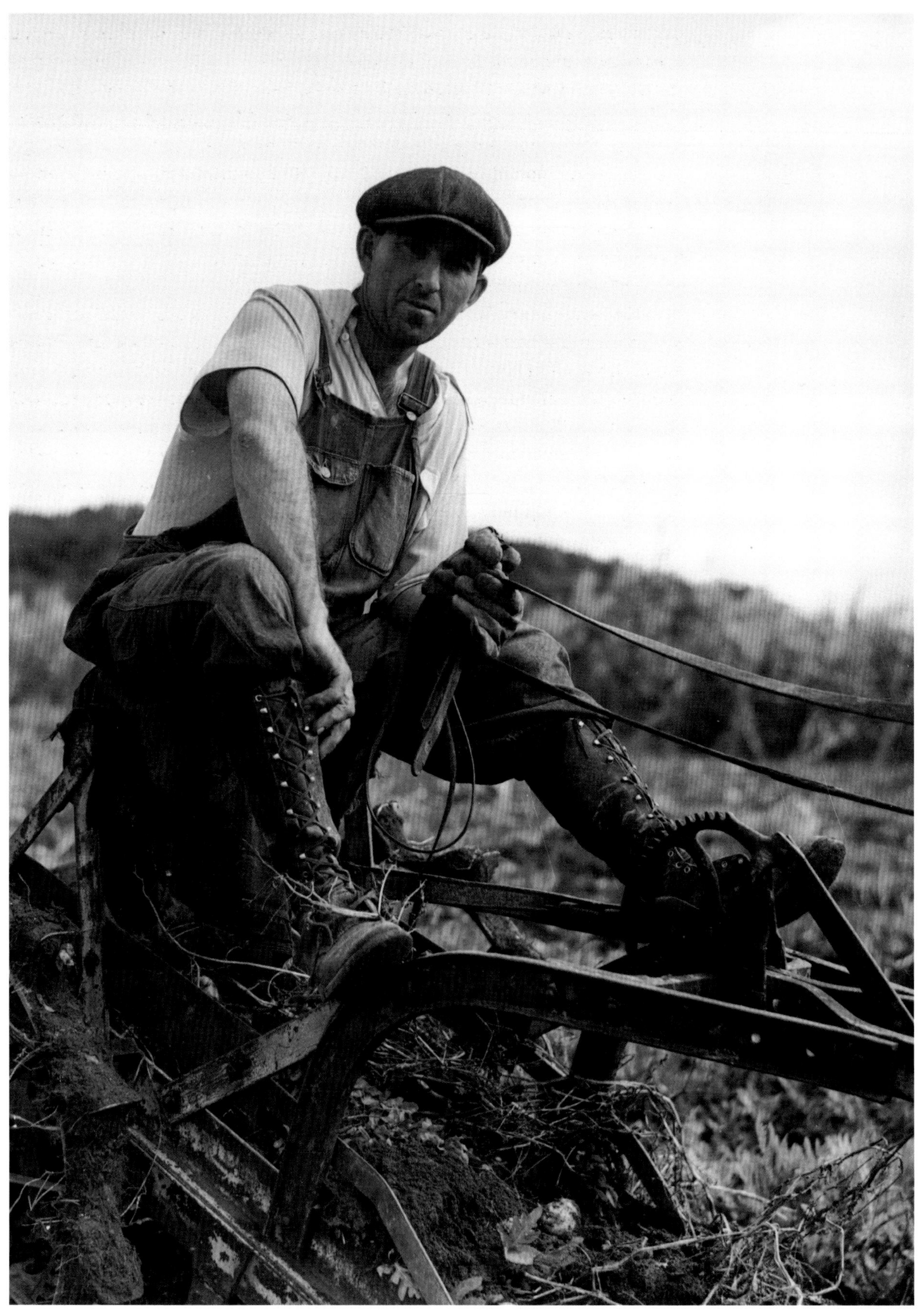

FIGURE 27 (opposite)
Jack Delano
Fairfield (vicinity), Vt. September 1941. William Gaynor, an FSA client who operates a dairy barn.

producing milk for the masses, starting in the field and moving "from the farm to the creamery to the railroad car."[38] In a later letter informing his boss that he had spent a day at the United Farmers Creamery in East Berkshire, one of the four farmers' cooperatives he visited in Vermont, Delano wrote that he continued "working on the milk angle," trying to document the whole process that put milk from rural areas on the tables of city families.[39] His documentation of the increasingly complicated processing of milk, from drop-off to testing to pasteurizing to bottling to shipping, puts to rest any nostalgia anyone might harbor about the simple pleasures of farm life. As Delano makes abundantly clear, here is a mass-produced product readied for market thanks to science and technology and the organized labor of business-savvy farmers.

Two other sets of farm or farm-related photographs occupied Delano during his stay in Vermont. One was general farm scenes, often landscapes, and the second was more intimate portraits of farm families at work. The landscapes are breathtaking: enormous, dramatic skies frequently fill more than half the frame, towering benignly over domesticated landscapes. Within these photographs, Vermonters, their tools, and their buildings are often consigned to minor roles, and often only a close viewing reveals the rocky lay of the land that is almost every Vermont farmer's hardship. However, somehow the effect, as in a haying scene captured outside of Brandon in August 1941, is not to diminish individuals but to celebrate their indomitability in a grand, impersonal universe.

Delano's more intimate portraits of Vermont farmers at work toy with time, compressing it, dissolving it, and leaving one confused about the state's cultural history. For example, photographs taken on this same trip depict a farmer in Windsor scything, just as farmers in Vermont did 150 years earlier; a farmer in Cambridge using a team of horses to gather hay in a scene that could as easily be 1841 as 1941; and a progressive farmer in Bellows Falls cutting hay with a tractor. The sequence is characteristic of Delano, who left Vermont with photographs to make almost any point Stryker might have wanted to make about Vermont and the state of American agriculture, at least in the Northeast. However, while these evocative photographs of farmers working with horses and hand tools, all frozen in single graceful moments stripped of chronological context, are easy to manipulate, they also make unwarranted suggestions about the state's innocence and imply that in the nation's backwaters there were still places in the garden where the machine had not yet infiltrated. As Delano himself knew inescapably after thoroughly working over the state, those rock-strewn farms were anything but Edens, and most of the men who sweated through their work with horses and calloused hands would happily have invested in labor-saving machinery if it had been within their power to do so.

Delano's intimate portraits of Vermont farmers at work are also complex artistic expressions. Trained as an artist, Delano approached all his documentary photography for the Historical Section not with the idea that his job was to photograph what was before his eyes but that his photographs needed to capture what he called "the essence of what you are seeing."[40] Clearly, when he visited farms and saw the work and commitment that farming required, he saw more than men at work in fields. In his photographs of farmers at work, as in all his other work for the Historical Section, he carefully orchestrated composition, value, and tone until he had achieved a formal balance that elevated photographs of activities as mundane as harvesting corn from work product to art (fig. 28).

Light was another of Delano's preoccupations. Unlike Russell Lee and Marion Post, who adapted to the infancy of flash photography, Delano sought out natural lighting wherever he could. When forced to shoot indoors, he used flash extensions to illuminate both background and foreground in order to create the effect of depth that more accurately reflected the scene. However, he preferred working in natural light, which he thought enabled him to capture not just the actuality of the scene but the "truth" of it. "It would often be the light that attracted me in the first place," he wrote in his memoir. "After all, it is sometimes the quality of the light that makes the difference between a simple documentary fact and a powerful statement about reality."[41] In his softly glowing farm portraits, which reflect his European studies of Rembrandt and Vermeer, Delano was able to capitalize on natural light and use it to dramatic effect. For example, his photographs of Isadore Lavictoire, a French Canadian farmer in Rutland, are among the few Vermont photographs in the file that dispel the impression of Yankee hegemony. Using light to emphasize the gaunt and worn features of the farmer's face and hands, they convince us that these are portraits not of a farmer but of a hard life.

Like Rembrandt, Delano was also drawn to the human face. No other Historical Section photographer in Vermont took as many portraits that eventually made their way into the file. Whether photographing a fiddle player at the World's Fair in Tunbridge, a young woman from the "girlie" show at the state fair in Rutland, or a group of older women gathered on a porch in East Albany for an auction, he demonstrated a rare sensitivity and respect for his subjects. His preference was to photograph in natural light using the kinds

FIGURE 28
Jack Delano
Hinesburg (vicinity), Vt. August 1941. Harvesting corn on a farm.

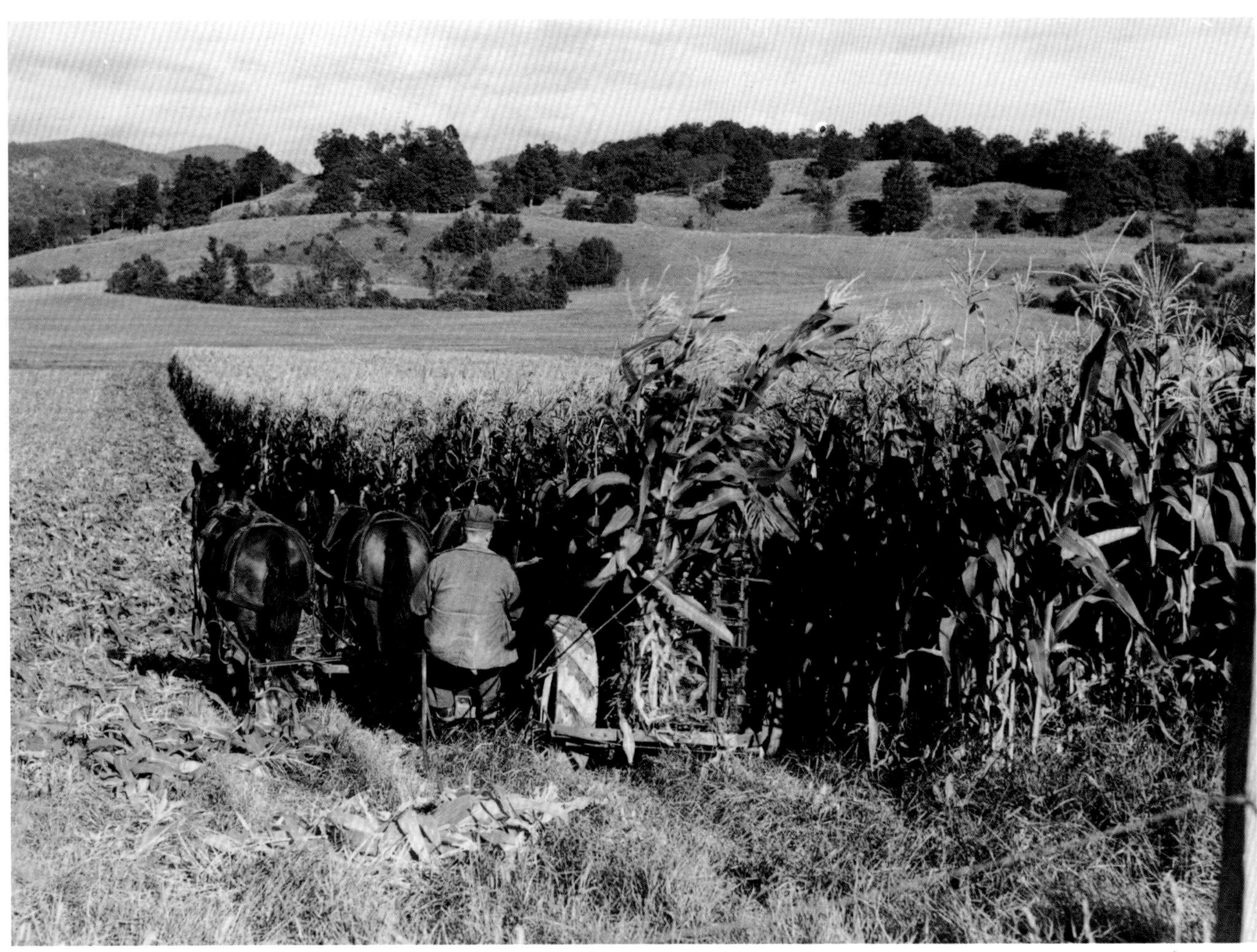

of backgrounds and props that speak for themselves and give the subjects a context that surpasses verbal description. The fiddler, for example, is playing his fiddle, as might be expected, but the portrait is of a man, mouth agape, eyes closed, fingers tense, momentarily transported by his music. The girlie, draped in her satin dress with its décolletage, is captured face on, in the direct way she is expected to perform. In both of these examples, Delano shows his understanding that in order to paint a true portrait of the fiddler, a common man, he had to be caught in the midst of performance, while in order to paint a true portrait of the girlie, a professional performer, he had to capture her off stage, in a private moment. The women at the auction, dressed in their better clothes, are a no-nonsense lot; those who have not turned their attention to the auction are scrutinizing the photographer with the kind of skepticism country people reserve for intruders.

Delano also photographed Vermont's small towns. Marion Post may have looked nostalgically at the passing innocence of rural life, but Delano displayed a broader vision for the state. He photographed a horse and buggy delivering mail in South Hero, but in general he trained his camera on scenes that were more socially complex: elderly gentlemen sitting on a bench overlooking the park in downtown St. Albans (fig. 29), women enjoying a lawn party in White River Junction, a farm family shopping in Rutland, boys relaxing on the green in Enosburg. The settings may be a combination of old and new, but the essential activity is timeless. He brought to these and other scenes like them a poignant intimacy, as if the subjects have been caught for eternity, not posed but being their quiet, everyday selves.

He could bring the same feeling to the inanimate towns as well. When he photographed the aging Hinesburg General Store with its prominent gas pumps, for example, he showed his sensitivity to the cultural clashes of modern times. Similarly, when he photographed the Fletcher Grange Hall standing cheek by jowl with the Congregational Church and looking almost indistinguishable from it, he showed his sensitivity to irony and nuance. In addition, he was able to capture photographs of village life that he seemed to recognize represented windows into the future: a chauffeur standing beside a car; a policeman directing traffic in Brattleboro; a modern, glass and steel apartment building; and an "Aluminum for Defense" scrap pile in Windsor. The latter may be the first official Historical Section, World War II photograph taken in Vermont.

Delano was also alert to specific ways in which the perception of Vermont was changing. As many of the state's hill towns were just beginning to emerge from a century of economic and social stagnation, Vermont was rediscovered by a nation searching for places and objects that connoted stability and tradition. Unlike the Vermont tourism of the late nineteenth century, which drew visitors to a landscape combining pastoral domestication and genteel recreational opportunities, Vermont tourism in the late 1930s and early 1940s appealed to the needs of a country recoiling from painful change. Here was a place that had changed relatively little. Some, such as Irene Delano, criticized what she saw:

> The lack of originality of these Vermonters is amazing. Every fifty yards along the highway we have seen stands selling "pure Vermont maple products." You can get maple sugar in the shape of a man, a leaf, a heart, a barrel, a dog, a circle, a house and on forever . . . but only maple sugar. Then they all seem to sell the same kind of "made in Vermont" baskets . . . but always the same kind.[42]

Delano, however, recognized more complex dynamics at play. Indeed, he recognized the very sameness his wife criticized as part of the state's appeal. Early in his trip, leaving Springfield, which struck him as an unattractive industrial town devoid of visitors, he wrote to his boss, "in almost every other place I've been[,] tourists were swarming everywhere. Most of them are from New York and New Jersey." Rather than being irritated by the masses, he was intrigued by the growing number of hill farms being converted to tourist and summer homes for middle-class visitors seeking refuge in Vermont. "I am going to spend a few days at one of those 'tourist' farms that takes in boarders during the summer," he continued in the same letter. "I passed one the other day where the boarders were playing croquette [*sic*] out on the front lawn."[43]

Jack Delano stayed with the Historical Section for almost two more years, but his assignments never again took him to New England. In late November 1941 Stryker sent Delano on a several-week visit to the U.S. Virgin Islands and to FSA projects in Puerto Rico. On 27 August 1943 he was drafted into the Army Corps of Engineers as a government photographer. After the war he and Irene returned to Puerto Rico, where they lived for most of the rest of their lives. Delano eventually became head of Puerto Rican educational television. However, he never abandoned photography, and he returned eventually to his artistic roots—music and art. In 1964 Jack and Irene Delano returned to New England to visit the places they had visited twenty-three years earlier. Almost everywhere they went, Delano was struck by how "rich" the region had become, how much the poor pockets of New England he had photographed had been transformed by the war and the era of prosperity that followed their visit in 1941. The exception was Vermont, which he felt had been bypassed by this regional good fortune. In Vermont, he recalled later, "things seemed very much the same as I had remembered them, except for the skiing and tourism."[44]

In the early decades of the twentieth century, Henri Cartier-Bresson, a French photographer, helped pioneer candid photography by developing a technique that was called "the decisive moment,"[45] which, for the most part, ignored great moments and instead sought out the ordinary, intimate details of day-to-day life. Delano readily acknowledged his debt to Cartier-Bresson and others, such as Robert Capa, who made him aware of the richness of the human experience around him.[46] His work for the Historical Section also opened his eyes to his country's culture. He said in an interview:

> To me it was a tremendous revelation of the tremendous variety of nationalities and the cultures within the cultures—the culture of a migratory worker as against someone from a New England town. All that kind of thing was completely new to me and just absolutely fascinating—to see how much the environment of a particular community affected the kind of people who lived in it.[47]

No doubt it was Delano's fascination, combined with his respect for the people he was photographing, that made his contribution to the section's file so special. "I just don't think," Irene Delano said in an interview, "there was a time that we worked for the FSA, or Jack did, that he just wasn't completely absorbed in it, and felt—as I know I did—that we were performing a great mission."[48]

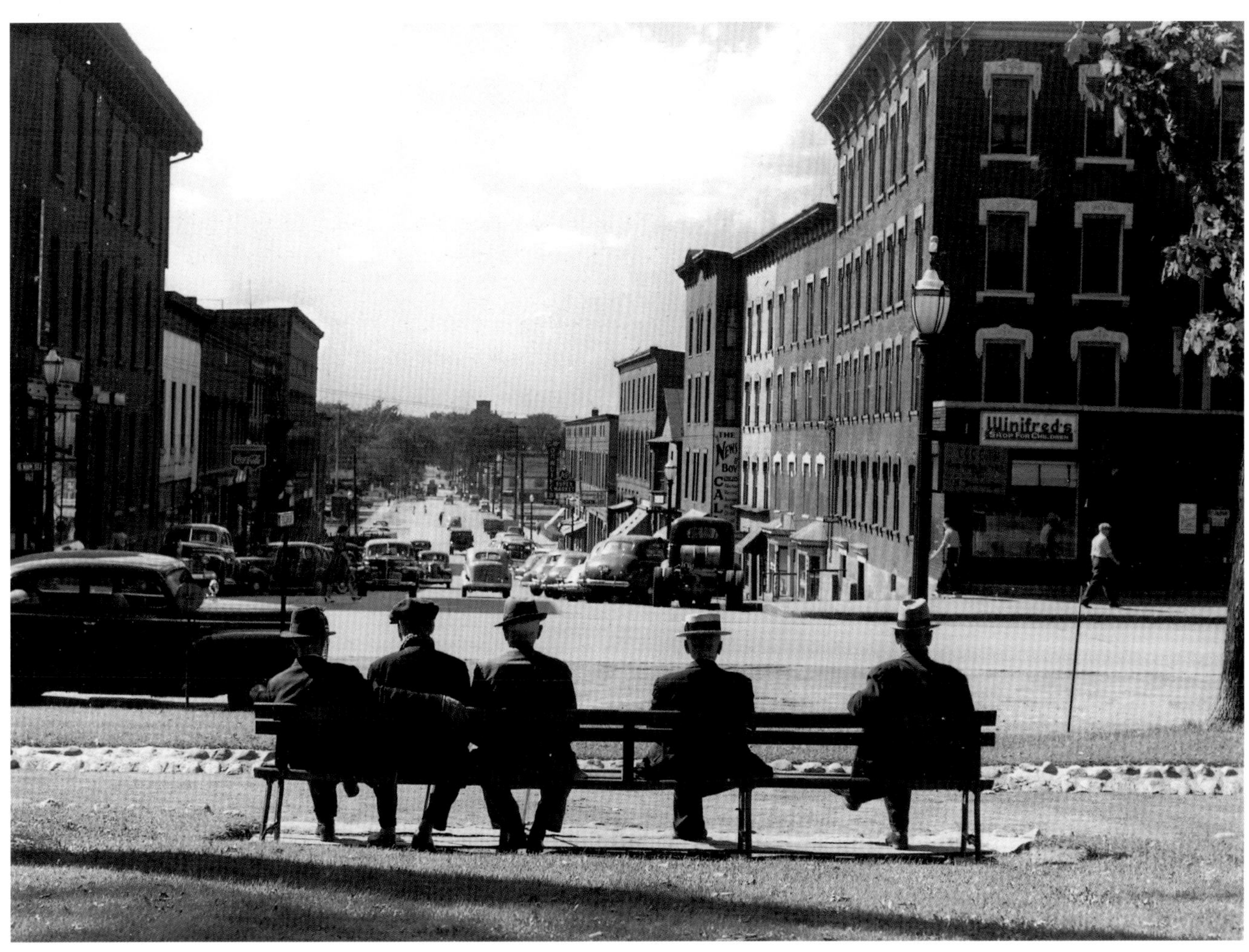

FIGURE 29

Jack Delano

St. Albans, Vt. August 1941. In the square, facing the Main St.

NOTES

1 / Lee to Stryker, 1 August 1940.

2 / Delano, *Photographic Memories*, p. 54.

3 / Ibid., pp. 49, 54.

4 / Delanos interview, p. 42.

5 / Stryker and Wood, p. 16.

6 / Delanos interview, p. 42.

7 / Delano, *Photographic Memories*, p. 1.

8 / Ibid., p. 15.

9 / Ibid., p. 18.

10 / Ibid., p. 19.

11 / Ibid., p. 21.

12 / Ibid.

13 / Ibid., p. 23.

14 / Ibid., p. 28.

15 / Delanos interview, p. 2.

16 / Delano, *Photographic Memories*, p. 28.

17 / O'Neal, 234.

18 / Stryker to Delano, 28 March 1940.

19 / Delanos interview, p. 4.

20 / Ibid., p. 27.

21 / Ibid., p. 6.

22 / Ibid.

23 / Delano, *Photographic Memories*, p. 49.

24 / Stryker to Delano, 12 September 1941.

25 / Delano to Stryker, 9 September 1941.

26 / Delano to Stryker, 8 August 1941.

27 / Delano kept in close contact with Stryker, and recorded his travels to his boss in letters dated 8 August, 11 September, and 12 September 1941. In its "Community Notes" of 11 September 1941, the *Randolph Herald and News* also mentioned Delano's presence at the Rutland fair.

28 / Delano to Stryker, 8 August 1941.

29 / Delanos interview, p. 14.

30 / Delano to Stryker, 23 September 1941.

31 / Ibid.

32 / Delano to Stryker, 9 September 1941.

33 / Delano to Stryker, 23 September 1941.

34 / "Community Notes," p. 4.

35 / Delano, *Photographic Memories*, p. 57.

36 / Caption sheet, FSA archive, Library of Congress. On the caption sheet, "Lavictiore" is probably a misspelling of the French Canadian name "Lavictoire."

37 / Ibid.

38 / Delano to Stryker, 9 September 1941.

39 / Delano to Stryker, 23 September 1941.

40 / Delanos interview, p. 22. .

41 / Delano, *Photographic Memories*, pp. 50–51.

42 / Irene Delano to Stryker, 4 August 1941.

43 / Delano to Stryker, 8 August 1941.

44 / Delanos interview, p. 45.

45 / Boatz, p. 113.

46 / Delanos interview, p. 55.

47 / Ibid., p. 43.

48 / Ibid.

Fritz Henle and Al Freeman

Two Historical Section photographers—Fritz Henle and Al Freeman—visited Vermont during 1942 before the section's office closed, but neither was on the same mission as those who had come before. Little is known about either trip except that both were brief, the purposes focused, and the territory they covered limited. Their photographs were probably never intended to be exhibited, and the use to which these images were eventually put comes closer to photojournalism, literally, if not aesthetically, than that of any of the Vermont work that preceded them.

Fritz Henle went to West Danville, Marshfield, and East Montpelier in June 1942, seven months after the United States entered World War II, to photograph war preparedness for the Historical Section, now a part of the U.S. Office of War Information. Henle was a surprising choice for a photographer on assignment in conservative northern Vermont just after the nation's entry into the global conflict. Born in Germany in 1909, he graduated from the School of Photography in Munich in 1931. An assignment for the camera company Rollei brought him to the United States in 1936, and he quickly landed a job with *Life*, where he worked with Alfred Eisenstadt developing new techniques in fashion photography that he would later use in work for *Harper's Bazaar*, *Town & Country*, and *Holiday*.[1] After the war, he globe-trotted as a freelance photographer, simultaneously writing a highly respected column for *Popular Photography* and producing approximately twenty books, including several on the use of Rollei cameras.[2] However, for three years during the war, he had an unlikely job as a photographer for the OWI.

Throughout the Historical Section's existence, its photographers had faced suspicion in some of the more remote areas they visited. Less than a year after Russell Lee visited Vermont, he wrote to Stryker that he had been mistaken for a German spy while on assignment and had to be rescued by the local sheriff.[3] As the nation became increasingly committed to the war, Historical Section photographers pressed for increasingly official-looking identification, possibly including fingerprints on a card, which they could present to wary authorities to assuage local anxieties over their presence and their cameras.[4] Now Henle, a German in the United States a brief six years, was sent to northern Vermont.

If Henle encountered any suspicion in West Danville, it did not stop him from fulfilling his assignment. At the West Danville store, he captured, in a series of photographs, the effect of the war on rural communities: a woman (instead of a man) delivering mail, a farmer reading a postcard informing him that last year's hired hand would not be returning because he had enlisted in the navy (fig. 30), two boys reading air raid instructions, a woman purchasing price-controlled items (fig. 31). The information accompanying the photographs in this series exemplifies the blatant propaganda that made these captions unlike any of the hundreds of Vermont captions that came before them. One caption quotes G. S. Hastings, owner of the West Danville store:

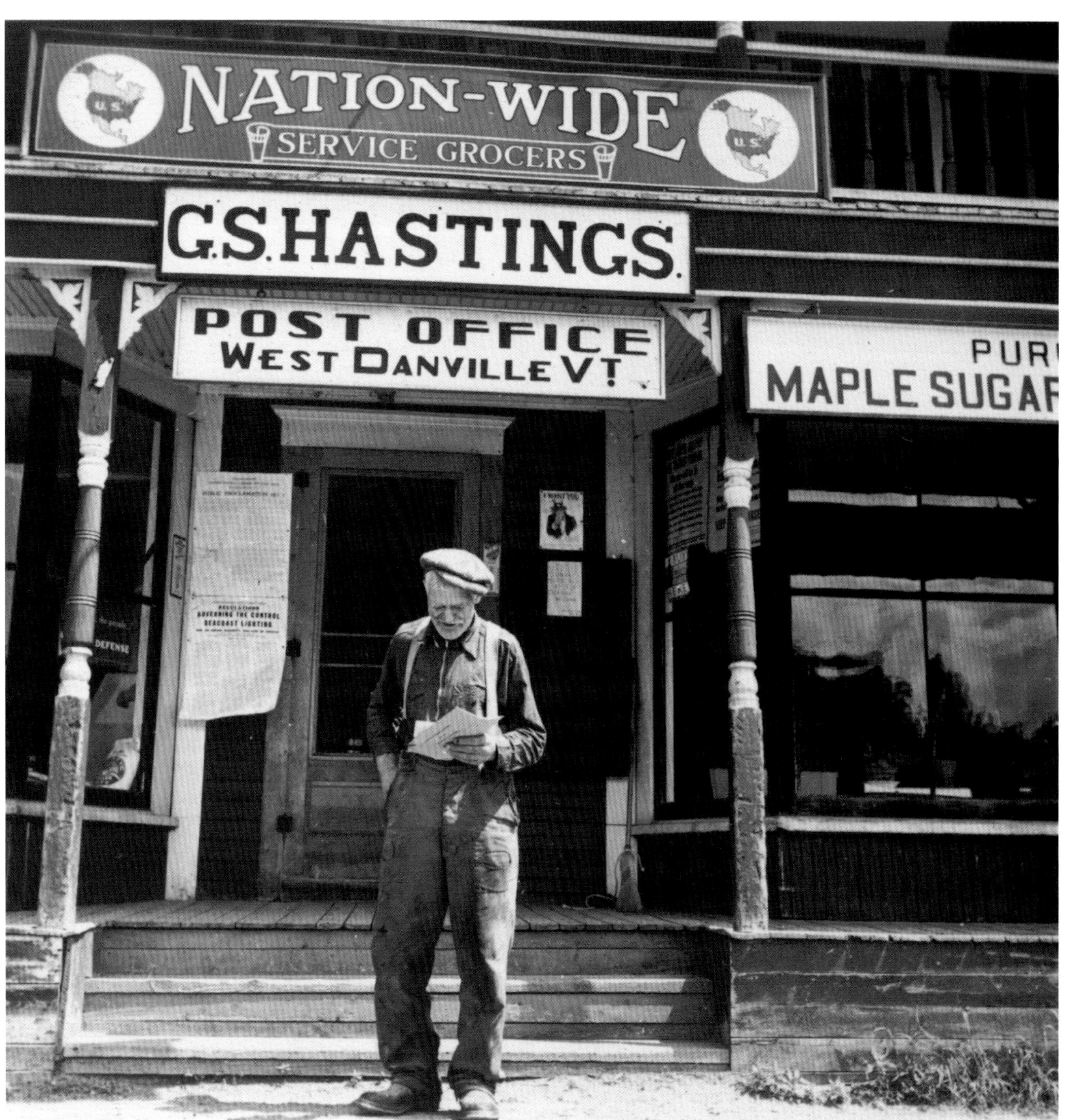

FIGURE 30

Fritz Henle

West Danville, Vt. July 1942. Frank Goss, 71-year-old farmer, in front of Gilbert S. Hastings's general store and post office reading his mail, which includes a card saying that his last year's hired man "won't be around for haying this year on account of he's in Californi' in the Navy."

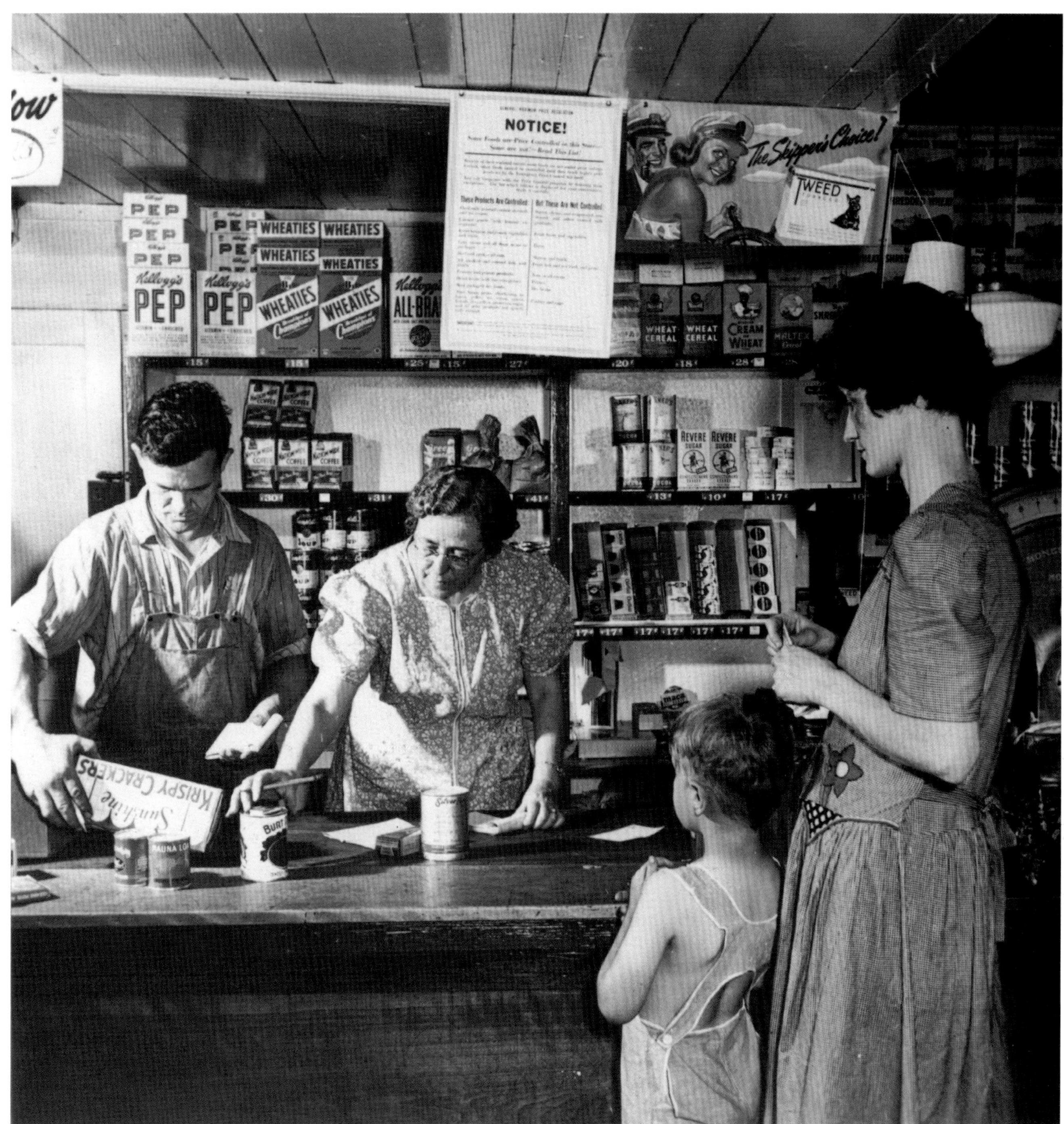

FIGURE 31

Fritz Henle

West Danville, Vt. July 1942. "What else will it be today, Mrs. Metcalf?" asks Mrs. Hastings who has clerked in the general store, owned by Mr. and Mrs. Hastings, for 29 years. Ronald Drown is looking on.

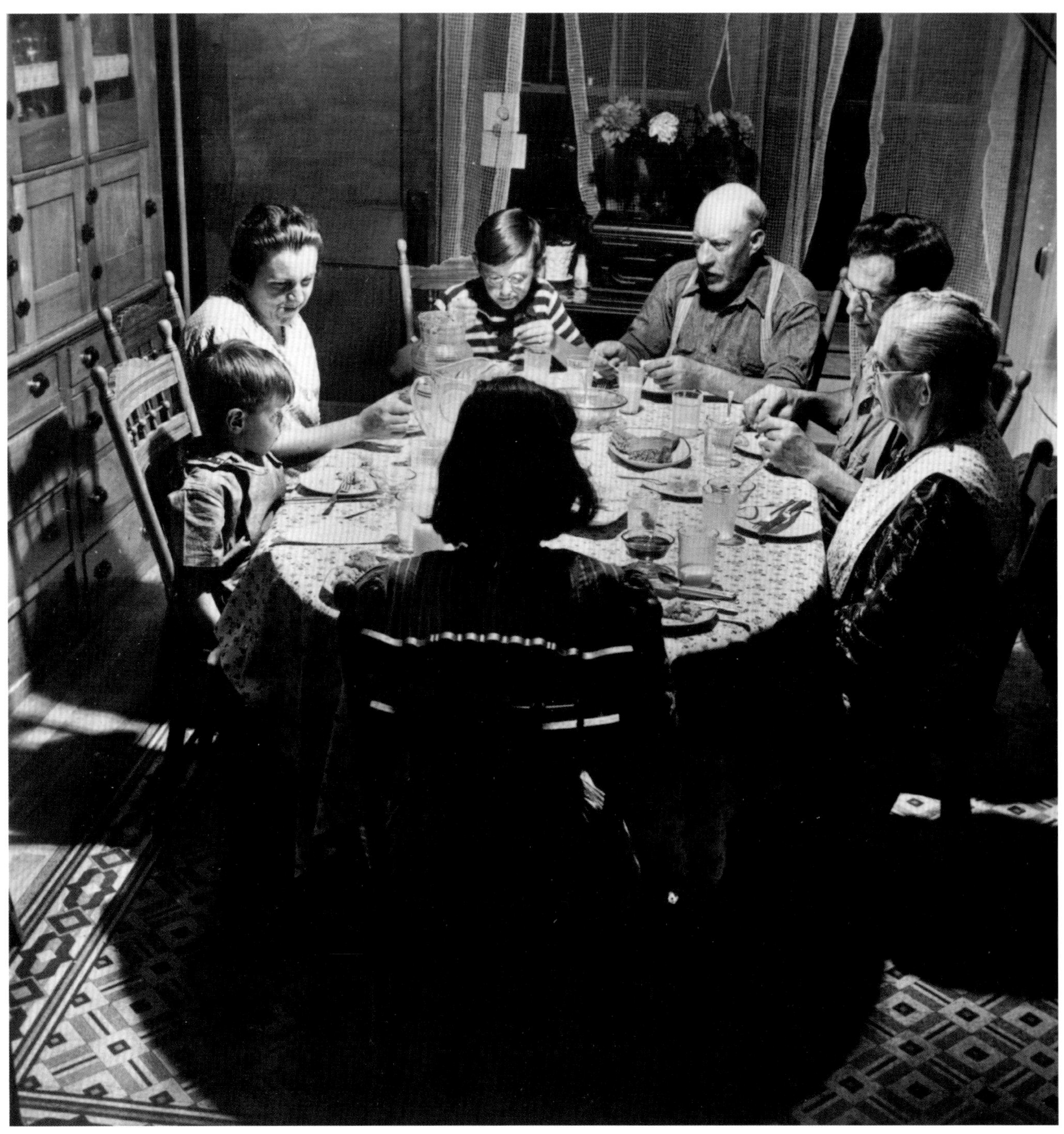

FIGURE 32
Fritz Henle
East Montpelier, Vt. July 1942. The Charles Ormsbee family at dinner.

You can't carry on a business, especially nowadays, without a lot of book work. But whether it is for income taxes or for making up price lists for cost-of-living commodities, it is all a part of keeping our government going so we can win the war and have the kind of world we want to live in.[5]

Henle also visited the Orton farm in Marshfield and the Charles Ormsbee farm in East Montpelier (fig. 32). Although the Historical Section file records the date of Henle's visit to the Ormsbees as July 1942, Myrtle Ormsbee, Charles's wife, kept a diary, now in the possession of her children, that notes otherwise. According to the entry for 13 June, "A photographer took pictures of us this P.M. They were getting pictures showing the average farm family in the war effort. They took lots of pictures of us at different tasks."[6]

Two of the Ormsbee children Henle photographed, Conrad and Marilyn, are still living and remember the visit. They believe their family's 175-acre farm was chosen for the assignment because their forty-year-old father, a third-generation farmer on that land, then milking twenty-five Jerseys, was known as an innovator. Active in the Farm Bureau, he also participated in the Farm Security Administration's Agricultural Conservation Program and helped oversee the war-imposed rationing of farm equipment for area farmers. Furthermore, he manned an army air observation post located in an old playhouse on the family's property.

As the Ormsbees recall, the well-orchestrated shooting session combined both carefully posed and casually posed photographs, but nothing approaching anything candid. Charles Ormsbee is shown contributing to the war effort by cutting lumber from trees on his land and later by milking his Jersey herd, which he had agreed to increase in size to aid the Food for Freedom program. He had also collected one and a half tons of steel, fifty pounds of it as discarded license plates, from neighboring farms. The children were shown doing their part as well. According to this series of photographs, eleven-year-old Conrad was raising a calf to help swell the herd and increase production, five-year-old Richard was licking savings stamps and pasting them into books, and fourteen-year-old Marilyn was learning through her 4-H group "to sew and cook economically and well." Even Myrtie Ormsbee, Charles's mother, demonstrates her part, knitting sweaters for the Red Cross.

Conrad and Marilyn Ormsbee remember well how irked their grandmother was by the false notes of some of these posed photographs. Richard was asked to don his dress shoes, which he would not normally have worn except to church and school. The Ormsbee house, for another example, had a pleasant, screened-in porch across its front, but because the screening limited the light, Henle asked Myrtie Ormsbee to pose on the back porch in her rocking chair and good clothes, including her best shoes, a situation that she found absurd and embarrassing. To add insult to injury, he recorded her name as Myrtle rather than Myrtie in the caption for every photograph in which she appears.[7]

Exactly one week after Henle appeared on the farm, according to Myrtle Ormsbee's diary, he asked the Ormsbees to come to Montpelier to see the photographs. Through some arrangement, they received prints of several of the photographs, including at least one that did not make it into the file, thus raising the question of whether others who were photographed over the years by the Historical Section photographers were also given prints in thanks for their cooperation.[8]

By late July, sets of photographs of the G. S. Hastings store and the Ormsbee farm, with accompanying articles composed by anonymous government writers in Washington, were being circulated to newspapers around the country. In Vermont the distributor was Harold Bergman, Branch Information Officer for the Vermont Office of Emergency Management, with offices in the old Pavilion Hotel in Montpelier.[9] Henle's photographs illustrated a story about how shortages of gasoline, tires, and cash were keeping away the tourists who had once sustained this popular summer camp area. However, the bigger point, and the one most reflective of Henle's pictures of proprietor Hastings waiting on customers inside his general store, was that ceiling prices imposed by the federal government were keeping

FIGURE 33 (opposite)
Al Freeman
Hardwick, Vt. 1942.
A few of the hundreds of items being donated and sold at the Victory Store, the money from which goes into a local war fund.

commodity costs low enough to feed families living in depressed areas, such as West Danville, that were unable to capitalize on wartime industry. The photographs and the accompanying article tried to offer proof of the wisdom of the government's wartime policies by demonstrating both their effectiveness in attending to domestic needs and their success in rallying support for the war, even among those far removed from the conflict.

The Ormsbee family, in a second article, was held up to the nation as a symbol of its most sacred values. "To these sturdy Vermonters the Four Freedoms of the Atlantic Charter seem as normal and natural a part of life as breathing the pure air of their Green Mountains," the author wrote. According to the article, Vermont's long history of opposing slavery, granting universal male suffrage, and tolerating diverse religions made it a beacon for those who believed in the freedoms President Franklin D. Roosevelt had expressed in his State of the Union address on 6 January 1941: freedom of speech, freedom of religion, freedom from want, and freedom from fear. Bergman claimed the Ormsbees' Yankee heritage made them naturally skeptical of Hitler's "lies" about the country's weaknesses and the death of democracy. Moreover, the family's history of independence and industry were the reasons why the Ormsbees were able to manifest their confidence in the country's ultimate victory by doing everything from adding cows to their Jersey herd to increasing milk production to canning vegetables to licking savings stamps to serving on the County Agricultural Planning Committee, an adjunct of the state's civil defense organization.

Both articles were reproduced in their entirety, accompanied by Henle's photographs, in at least one Vermont newspaper. The *Burlington Free Press* ran the Ormsbee profile as a "Special to the *Free Press*" on 5 August 1942; the G. S. Hastings store article ran, without a byline, three days later. These articles are flag-waving propaganda, exhorting those who read them to patriotic fervor. However, the Ormsbee article is remarkable because it promotes themes that had been evolving since the late nineteenth century, when Vermonters began emerging from their isolation and quite unexpectedly found themselves on a national stage, imbued with such exceptional personal qualities as independence, resilience, resourcefulness, and industry. In perpetuating this stereotype, Henle and Bergman lent credibility to Norman Rockwell's decision two years later to use his fellow Vermonters to illustrate the Four Freedoms in a series of paintings and posters that were widely successful and carried this stereotyped image of Vermont to the country's farthest corners.

Like Henle, Al Freeman made the final Historical Section visit to Vermont under the auspices of the OWI. Arriving in October 1942, Freeman, like Henle, kept his stay short and visited only two locations. One of the stops was Hardwick, which Carl Mydans had visited six years earlier in the heat of the 1936 election season. This time the subject was the town's Victory Store, a sprawling, eclectic collection of donations of everything from ducks, puppies, and produce to crutches, beds, and commodes, all of which were being sold to raise money for the war effort. The signage says everything: "War Fund Sale," " Save War Fats for Explosives," "Give Your Salvage/Save Your Country."[10] In a compressed form, the photographs trace the process of receiving donations, displaying them, and selling them to families that cart them away in buggies and automobiles (fig. 33).

Seven months passed before anything was done with these photographs, perhaps partly because the photographs themselves are not extraordinary, but just as likely because Hardwick's Victory Store closed during a harsh winter and did not reopen until spring. The man who made it possible for this story to move into the national consciousness was Fred M. Learned, Vermont Information Officer in the state's Office of War

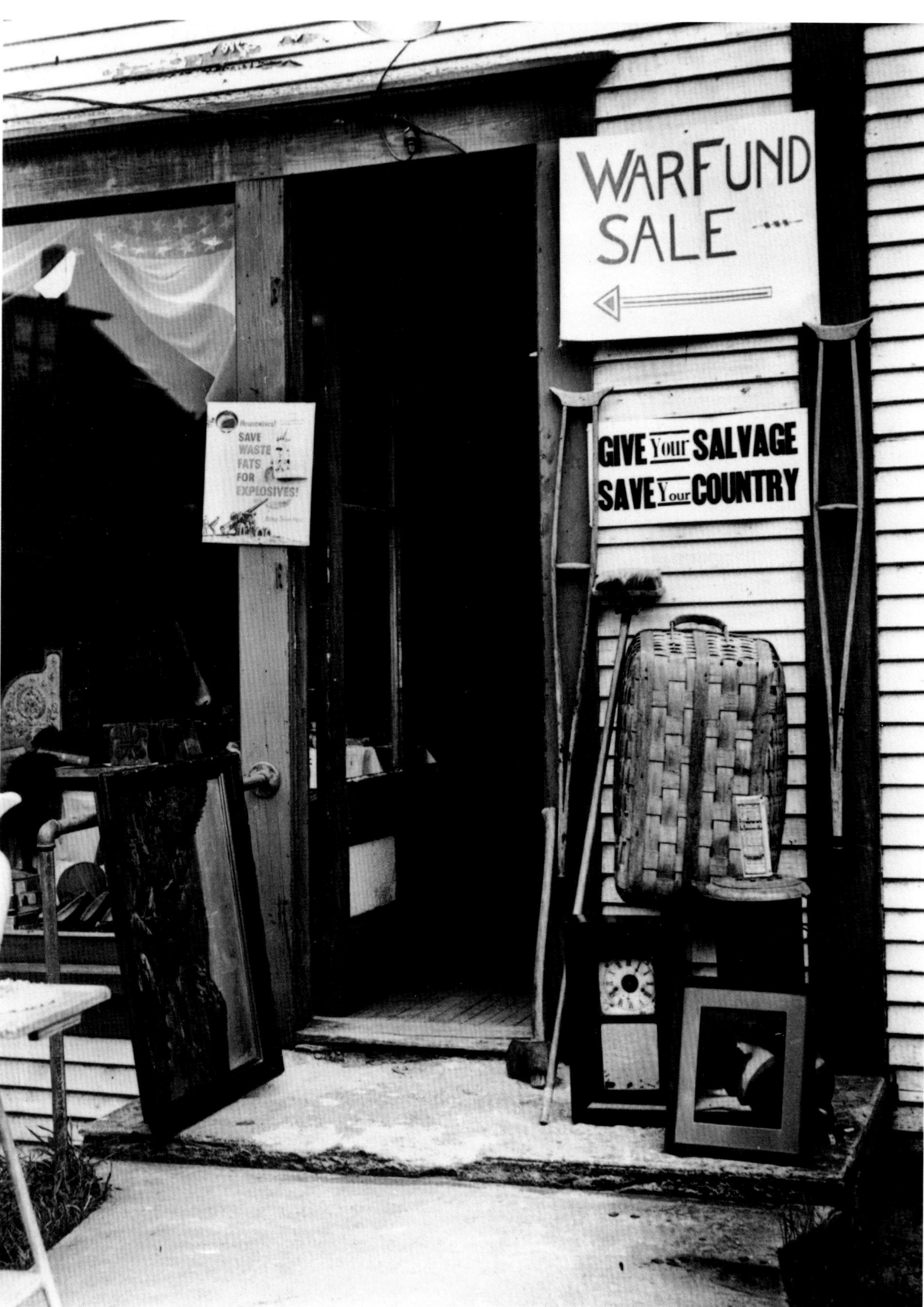
WAR FUND
SALE
GIVE Your SALVAGE
SAVE Your COUNTRY
SAVE
WASTE
FATS
FOR
EXPLOSIVES!

Information, located in the Pavilion Hotel in Montpelier. When months passed and the government still had not produced an accompanying article, Learned undertook to write one himself about Hardwick's Victory Store, leading with the line, "Yankee ingenuity is paying the war effort big dividends in Hardwick, Vermont." The story went on to explain that J. B. Grow, a resident of Hardwick, had started the store in 1942 after reading about a similar type of community fundraiser for the Red Cross in a small town in Canada. At the time the photographs were taken, twenty-six different community organizations were collaborating to operate the store, and its income—$1,500 during the summer of 1942—was helping to support everything from the Red Cross to the Army and Navy Relief Fund to the Vermont Blood Bank. Once he had completed the package, Learned suggested that the article and photographs be released to newspapers across the country. He also asked permission to release the story to Vermont newspapers.[11]

Sixty years later, the other set of photographs Freeman took on his visit are hard to find. These images of the Vermont Marble Company, in Proctor, documenting the conversion of equipment from marble finishing to metalworking, have their original catalogue numbers, and prints can be found in the section's extensive archive. However, they are not listed among the Vermont photographs in the Historical Section index. The irony is that these photographs, shot with a fine eye for composition and light, are by far the more interesting and dramatic of Freeman's images. Testaments to Yankee ingenuity, they explain—more satisfactorily than the Hardwick photographs do—why Freeman was sent five hundred miles north from Washington to take pictures in Vermont.

This was complex work: engineers at the marble works, after traveling around to visit nearby metalworking shops, had converted marble polishing machines to radial drills, a marble-turning lathe to a horizontal boring mill, circular planers to straight planers, and marble planers to metalworking planers. And their resourcefulness did not stop there. According to a fact sheet that accompanied the photographs,

> One of [the Vermont Marble Company's] customers shipped them a job to be planed which took a larger capacity than any of their planers could do. Being a Vermonter [and] not knowing what it was to be stuck, they took one right and one left open-side marble-working planer, put them together after completely rebuilding them, [and] tied the platen together, using it as one planer.[12]

A few of the marble workers are shown putting finishing touches on memorials, but clearly most of the firm's employees have joined the war effort. Long accustomed to working in marble with sixteenth-inch tolerances, they had become skilled metalworkers during the course of the two-year conversion, now operating with tolerances of one thousandth of an inch. Trained in the art of producing memorials and using equipment that had recently finished marble columns for the U.S. Supreme Court Building in Washington, they were now fabricating floors for battleships and marine-engine bases for Liberty Ships, the utilitarian cargo ships being mass-produced for the U.S. Navy.

Unlike most of the Historical Section photographers who preceded him, Freeman did not write his own captions. Contact prints were sent from Washington to Harold Bergman, in the Vermont Office of Emergency Management in Montpelier, at the request of the Vermont Marble Company, and Bergman was asked to obtain the correct caption material.

Perhaps this explains why the captions are unusually rich in personal information, containing not just the names of the men in the pictures, but their ages, often something about their work history, and sometimes something about their families, especially if anyone else in the extended family was engaged in war work.

By the time the last Historical Section photographer visited Vermont, the program was slipping from Stryker's control and losing the breadth that had given it its compelling message. Appropriated by other powers within the government as World War II forced the country to direct its considerable energies toward that single cause, the Historical Section had watched the ground shift from underneath it. Perhaps, too, the freshness of its approach had faded over the seven years of its existence. Although the aesthetics of the photography it nurtured would be a lasting legacy, many of the themes had lost their power to startle and move people, and were supplanted by new themes and a new crisis. When it officially closed, the Historical Section had become not a lens through which Americans could see opportunities for social and economic reform but a tool to instruct them of their wartime duties.

NOTES

1 / *Photographers Encyclopedie International.*

2 / *MacMillan Biographical Encyclopedia,* p. 272.

3 / Lee to Stryker, 14 June 1940.

4 / Lee to Stryker, 8 December 1941.

5 / Library of Congress, Prints and Photographs Division, print number LC-USF34-53827-E.

6 / Ormsbee diary, 13 June 1942.

7 / Ibid., 20 June 1942.

8 / Ormsbees interview.

9 / FSA archive, Library of Congress.

10 / Library of Congress, Prints and Photographs Division, print number LC-USF34-54137-D.

11 / Learned to Harry J. Coleman, memo and article, 12 May 1943. Coleman was News Editor, Division of Photography, Vermont Office of War Information.

12 / FSA archive, Library of Congress.

The Vermont Photographs in Perspective

In 1940 when Sherwood Anderson, Edwin Rosskam, and Roy Stryker collaborated on choosing photographs for Anderson's book *Home Town,* they chose 142 prints from the Historical Section's file of prints and negatives to illustrate the spirit of rural life in the United States. Vermont shines in this homage, represented by eleven photographs; only North Carolina has as many, and the other five New England states are represented by a total of three. The book's opening photograph, by Arthur Rothstein, shows the courthouse steeple and a church spire in Stowe, towering like twin guardians over a somnolent streetscape in bright sunshine. In the book's chronicle of the seasons, Vermont carries the entire section on winter, as if no other state had to endure months of snow and cold or had the pluck to survive them. Marion Post's seven photographs of Vermonters playing, working, and generally carrying on with their lives amid the snow and ice are both hauntingly beautiful and reassuring. Russell Lee's peaceful photograph of a man raking leaves beneath towering trees that must be nearly as old as the brick Greek Revival farmhouse in the background conveys a feeling of steadfastness and permanence that, like the other Vermont photographs in the book, projects an indelible image of the state and its people as independent, self-reliant, hardy, and imbued with common sense.

The idea of using photographs to convey a particular image of Vermont was more than fifty years old in 1940 when *Home Town* was published, but the message had evolved in distinct and ironic ways over that time. In the thirty years after the Civil War ended, published views of Vermont tended to fall into one of three categories, each of which was an antecedent to the Historical Section work. The most generic are the portraits, a parade of heads and high collars in the case of the women, and occasionally a full-length portrait of a man, especially if a uniform was involved. In almost all cases, there is virtually no context, no visual clue to help portray character, and certainly nothing to distinguish the state's foremost citizens from the leading lights in every other up-and-coming state. The point was clearly not to make Vermonters look like Vermonters, but to make them indistinguishable from the successful by any standard, in any state.

Booster photographs, which constitute a second category, derive from the same impulse that made bird's-eye views a lucrative business in the second half of the nineteenth century. These images of Vermont's industries and technological achievements—its bridges and railroads, its quarries and its well-established business districts—go a step further than the generic portraits in identifying Vermont, because the landscape was familiar to those who knew the state's lakes, mountains, towns, and cities. However, the emphasis in the photographs is not on the geography of Vermont, but rather on the machine in the garden. Aiming to convince the viewer that the state, though off the beaten path, was as accomplished in the industrial arts as other leading regions of the country, photographers went as far as possible to make it look like other progressive areas.

A third popular category of early photography in Vermont was genre photographs, which derived from scenes of country life in the late nineteenth century. Some were bucolic portrayals of rural life different only in medium, not theme, from late-nineteenth-century romantic paintings by Vermont painters such as Thomas Waterman Wood and Eastman Johnson. Others, showing, for example, a young woman in a long white dress playing croquet on the expansive lawn of a fine estate or resort, avoided the agrarian context but not the saccharin overtones. Once again, however, Vermont is the backdrop, not the theme. The photographer has focused the camera not on the state, but on a vanishing way of life, one that Americans, trembling before the social and economic implications of the industrial age, were beginning to regard with increasing sentimentality as the century approached its end.

All three types of photographs appear in the *Vermonter*, the state's first promotional magazine. Launched in August 1895, the *Vermonter* acknowledged in its introductory message to readers that "Vermonters have for a long time recognized the desirability of a magazine exclusively devoted to the interests of the State." The editor, Charles S. Forbes, went on to praise Vermont "as a favored land, [possessing] in a marked degree all that goes to make life comfortable, attractive and delightful," and as one proof of this claim pointed to the growing number of summer visitors drawn to Vermont's natural charms.[1] Although the editor makes no effort to solicit photographs, as he does articles, correspondence, and "items of news and personal notes," the magazine is subtitled *An Illustrated Monthly Magazine* and liberally employs portraiture, booster, and genre photography toward its ends, without in any way succeeding in visually portraying a distinctive state character.

However, the selling of Vermont began in earnest as the nineteenth century approached its end, and photography played an increasingly important part. The change was driven by two factors: Americans' fear that urbanization and industrialization were destroying values such as independence and self-reliance; and a subtle aesthetic shift from a worship of the sublime, or wild and dramatic, to an appreciation of the pastoral, with its soothing, domesticated rural views and Edenic associations. Vermont, still largely a backwater despite Charles Forbes's high praise for its accomplishments, was in a position to capitalize on both cultural trends. In 1891 the Vermont State Board of Agriculture published the "Resources and Attractions of Vermont," the first in a series of state-sponsored pamphlets that tried to make the best of difficult circumstances by advertising abandoned hill farms for sale to out-of-staters searching for a country refuge. Those pamphlets are important transitional publications. On the one hand, they continued to portray Vermont as a progressive state whose achievements were equal to (and no different from) those of any other state; but on the other hand, the photographs began to promote Vermont as a specific place distinctly different from the nation's growing urban areas. In these pictures, scene and site acquire new significance and distinguishing characteristics, and, thanks to the powers of photography, the message they sent is that Vermont is a place where rural values persevere and are ineluctably linked to a distinctive landscape.

When *Vermont Beautiful* was published in 1922, the book lavishly employed photography to further the claims that the state possessed uncommonly beautiful landscape and a unique relationship with the past. The inaugural publication in a series that would grow to include "the older or more beautiful states," this was the first major photography book on Vermont.[2] Wallace Nutting, of Massachusetts, the author and photographer, admitted a special affection for the state he had been visiting for twenty years and where he had spent five summers. He infused the photographs and their captions with a moral authority that was becoming distinctly associated with Vermont. "Unspoiled" and "untouched" read captions accompanying photographs of this New England arcadia, where the waters either drop dramatically over falls or lie like glass, reflecting their birch-lined banks, where country roads meander through thick woods and fields lie eternally peaceful under a noon-day sun. More interesting, however, are the genre photographs, in every one of which Nutting posed Vermonters in nineteenth-century garb, fishing, visiting, haying, carting hay with oxen, or riding to town in bonnets and buggies. The message of his caption "Home Sweet Home," accompanying a photograph of a worn but tidy old farmhouse tucked beneath towering maples with a buggy in the front yard, is unmistakable: virtue resides here.

Another Vermont photographer of the 1920s was using a camera to promote the same image. Clara Sipprell, born in Ontario and reared in Buffalo, New York, came to Thetford in 1917 and spent seventeen years there photographing her neighbors. Working with an 8 × 10 camera under the influence of Alfred Steiglitz's "pictoral" photography, she carefully composed her soft-focus, chiaroscurist images using symbolism and balance to idealize even harsh circumstances. The subjects are time travelers, caught in the present in a scene or performing work that makes an inescapable reference to a golden past. To enhance the suggestion that these wise elders are icons of a better, earlier time, light that is surreal and almost divine suffuses the scenes, making them luminous. As further proof of Sipprell's intention to soften any hard realities in her work, she sometimes printed her photographs on tissue paper. Vermont would be incidental to these portraits, mostly taken during the 1920s, except that at a time when post-World War I economics and politics were making the nation jittery and hungry for stability, Sipprell's images conveyed the idea that the values Americans sought were still part of the fabric of life in the Green Mountains.

Three more books that used photographs extensively to celebrate Vermont during these years deserve mention, and all were published in 1937. One was *And So Goes Vermont: A Picture Book of Vermont As It Is*, edited by Vrest Orton. Though short, it was the first book to rely solely on photographs and captions to convey its message, which Charles Beecher Hogan explained in the foreword was to "exhibit to those who do know and those who do not know Vermont what Vermont *really* [my emphasis] looks like, physically and morally."[3] The book's title is ironic, however, because the images were obviously so carefully and selectively chosen. Physically, the state is portrayed in these photographs primarily through classic architecture that emphasizes columns, spires, and the clean lines of early nineteenth-century building styles (complete with their allusions to a more virtuous political past); and through landscape, including sweeping vistas of unspoiled mountains, ripening fields, covered bridges, placid lakes, and tidy villages. Orton avoids all images of cities; rather, floating bridges and extensive barn complexes, farmhouses and tree-lined country roads portray an arcadia uncontaminated by automobiles, immigrants, poverty, or industrialization

The moral theme is heavy-handed. A preponderance of photographs of the elderly, and the character that is etched on their faces, reflects a lifetime of industry. For that matter, almost everyone in the book is engaged in some hard physical activity, from scything or shoveling snow by hand to haying with oxen to quarrying marble at Danby for the U.S. Supreme Court Building in Washington, D.C., to skiing and canoeing. Orton is not so puritanical in his focus that he avoids Vermonters enjoying themselves. He shows summer camps, country fairs, swimming holes, and family picnics, but the message is that the

American work ethic is still the driving moral force in Vermont, that its society has not been corrupted by the changing world outside its borders.

A second book published in 1937 was different in some ways but strikingly similar in others. *Vermont: A Guide to the Green Mountain State*, part of the American Guide Series written by workers of the Federal Writers' Project of the Works Progress Administration for the State of Vermont, was the product of a New Deal program designed to give jobs to unemployed writers. Unlike earlier books on Vermont, this was written to introduce outsiders to every corner of the state, and its extensive text even provided readers with detailed tours that included the state's growing cities and manufactories. Its tone, like that of all the WPA state guides, is promotional. However, neither the photography nor the opening essay, "Vermonters," written by the celebrated Vermont author Dorothy Canfield Fisher, could escape the growing trend to portray the state idealistically. Fisher even repeats a story about her godfather, who left Vermont for Kansas as a child and made his fortune there. She recalls that he often remarked that the entire state of Vermont should be made into a national park, which people could visit to see how their grandparents had lived.[4] The photographs, published anonymously, do little to disabuse anyone of the notion that Vermont is frozen in time. Vermonters themselves are practically nonexistent, but their towers and spires, their monuments and buildings with their classic lines, their neat farms and sleepy villages, all testaments to their values, bespeak days before most Americans had lost touch with the land and become part of the nation's uprooted manufacturing class.

Charles Edward Crane was the author of the third book, *Let Me Show You Vermont*, as well as of a later book, published in 1941, *Winter in Vermont*. In his introductory chapter to *Let Me Show You Vermont*, Crane wrote that he hoped to "reflect Vermont, in some of its phases, differently and more fully than has been done before," and some of the forty-three photographs he selected to illustrate his book—images of skiers and of a granite quarry in Barre, for example—succeed in doing this. In the end, however, his choice of Clara Sipperell's images of elderly Vermonters, Herbert Congdon's exquisite but timeless portraits of Vermont's classic architecture, and a preponderance of pastoral landscapes and sleepy townscapes perpetuates the stereotype rather than rebutting it. Instead, it was Crane's second book, *Winter in Vermont*, published just four years later, that begins to add real dimension to any portrait of the state. For one thing, it demonstrates the profound influence the Historical Section's photographic aesthetic was having on photography . The eighty-nine photographs in *Winter in Vermont* are rife with images of activity, from skating to skiing to ice boating. A half dozen images are glamour shots, portraits of well-known skiers visiting Mount Mansfield, all photographed by Louise Dahl-Wolfe of *Harper's Bazaar*. Another half dozen are Marion Post's images, taken during her sojourn to the state in the winter of 1940 and distributed, as were thousands of other Historical Section photographs, to publications that became part of Roy Stryker's vast outreach effort. The aesthetic change in four years is remarkable. People now appear abundantly, not as props but as subjects, each in a context and each unmistakably in the moment. The potential in such a photography to bring to the nation a more realistic perception of Vermont was enormous, but ultimately it was undermined by Crane's goals, which were just as promotional as those of the authors who came before him, and which, therefore, precluded a true picture of Vermont in all its complexity.

Vermont: A Profile of the Green Mountain State, published in 1941 by the Works Progress Administration and sponsored by the University of Vermont in collaboration with the

Vermont Writers' Project, reinforces how easy it was to adopt the aesthetic of the Historical Section while falling short of its vision. This small chapbook, part of the American Pictorial Guide Series, contains little text but is abundantly illustrated with photographs by Historical Section photographers and others. The book is noteworthy for demonstrating how little the attitudes toward Vermont had changed in four years, and for continuing—deliberately and self-consciously—to promote Vermont and the idea that Vermonters "have held fast to the ways of their fathers, and perhaps in so doing have preserved on their small farms and in their quiet villages something valuable that might otherwise be lost in the larger pattern of American life."[5] However, the photographs are noteworthy for another reason, as well. The book—which opens with an image by an unnamed photographer of an elderly man sitting and reading a newspaper beneath a portrait of Abraham Lincoln—is persuasive evidence of the success and growing popularity of documentary photography, with its hallmark emphases on people, environmental context, and careful composition. Other photographs in this volume, taken from the archives of the *Rutland Herald*, the Vermont Marble Company, the Howe Scale Company, or the portfolios of half a dozen individuals, all reflect the documentary vocabulary honed by photographers for the Historical Section, but none ultimately demonstrates the social conscience and passion for change that drove section photographers into the field and kept them there for seven years.

A single photographer during the twenty years that preceded the depression showed a different side of Vermont, one that also served as an antecedent for some of the Historical Section's finest work. Lewis Hine, who had done pioneering work photographing immigrants at Ellis Island between 1904 and 1909, joined the staff of the National Child Labor Committee in 1908 and traveled the country for ten years photographing working conditions that stripped children of their health and childhood. His work was influential; by 1918 Congress had passed legislation outlawing the worst child labor.[6] In 1930 he was hired to document the construction of the Empire State Building, and by the latter 1930s, he was trying, unsuccessfully, to get a job with Roy Stryker in the Historical Section. He never succeeded, however, perhaps because he was considerably older than the photographers Stryker generally hired or perhaps because Hine was known to use pejorative adjectives such as "slovenly" in his captions, and Stryker demanded a much higher degree of sensitivity in his photographers.

Yet Hine's early work was seminal and influenced the work of the Historical Section.[7] Notwithstanding his later differences with Stryker, Hine took striking portraits of children in their environment, in fields or factories or on street corners, and often used a rich contrast of light and shadow to help dramatize the heartbreaking story of an innocence and a potential lost. In Vermont, he took at least forty-six photographs of children working in cotton and wool mills, on farms, in marble quarries and lumber mills, or selling newspapers on the city's streets. The children's bare feet and torn clothes say as much about their situation as their frank gazes say about their spirit. The photographs are memorable for publicizing a side of Vermont that no one had ever before photographed. They are remarkable as well for portraying an ethnic group, specifically the growing numbers of French Canadians, who before this time were rarely recorded in the state's official photography and who are barely represented in the Historical Section's photographs of Vermonters. Ultimately, however, these photographs do not distinguish Vermont from any other place. Rather, the photographs reveal the universal oppression of child labor and link Vermont to the anonymous and increasingly industrial world beyond its borders.

Into this complex photographic mix of Vermont's iconography, Stryker stirred the geography lessons of consecutive editions of J. Russell Smith's *North America*, the book Stryker instructed all the Historical Section photographers to read before they set out on their road trips. Stryker loved all publications that used illustrations creatively, a love that was rooted in his first assignments at Columbia, but he especially admired Smith's innovative textbooks, in which photographs provided not just graphic variety on a page but a visual, didactic corollary to the text. Unfortunately, only the use of graphics was progressive; too often the message in Smith's books is a distressing mix of eugenics, racism, prejudices, and social Darwinism. Successive editions of the book are full of disturbing claims—for example, that the southern climate saps the strength of white men and that Native Americans are unable to compete with Europeans because of an inability "to stand the pain of steady work."[8]

Smith's underlying thesis, however, has stood the test of time: people live in unique, identifiable places whose natural resources shape their lives and living. Vermont, in his view, was a hardscrabble place where hill farms were being abandoned and purchased by summer tourists; where indiscriminate logging had stripped the mountains of their primary resource, leaving farmers without an occupation to sustain them through the winter; where maple sugaring rounded out a profitable farm year; where abundant good hay in the Champlain and Connecticut river valleys could support dairy farmers whose highly perishable milk nourished the burgeoning cities of southern New England; where the glaciers had left behind rock good for quarrying; and where modernization was needed to sustain agriculture against many odds. However, Smith was as susceptible as anyone to the idealization of the difficult. In the 1942 edition of *North America*, Smith and his co-author, Ogden Phillips, devote a long passage to quoting Dorothy Canfield Fisher on the moral fortitude of Vermonters:

> Vermont, like some of the remote valleys of the Pyrenees, has always been too far out of the furiously swirling current of modern industrial life to be much affected by it or to dread its vagaries. . . . I am afraid there is an element of pride in the granite-like comfort they take in the security given them by their plain tastes and ability to deal with life first hand.[9]

This picture of Vermont, as drawn by authors and photographers over the previous forty years, and perhaps epitomized by a popular photograph from the 1920s of Vermont-born President Calvin Coolidge wearing his grandfather's woolen smock and scything hay, would have been what the Historical Section photographers were looking for when they crossed over the border from New Hampshire or Massachusetts. However, as Russell Lee's photographs of brutal poverty, Arthur Rothstein's photographs of exhausted threshers, and Jack Delano's photographs of Vermont town and city life attest, reality tempered expectation. The section photographers quickly discovered that Vermont in the late 1930s and early 1940s was more complex than anyone had succeeded in portraying so far. For one thing, according to Vermont historian Paul Gillies, Vermonters generally took less notice of the depression because conditions were not that different from those they had been facing for the past century. Unquestionably, by the time the Historical Section photographers began visiting Vermont, many communities in the state had been in decline for decades. Between 1880 and 1930, the population of the United States had grown by 250 percent; the population of New England had grown by one hundred percent; but the population of Vermont had grown by only eight percent.[10] Although some urban pockets were thriving, two hundred of the state's 240 towns were on a slow, seemingly irreversible decline that left fields growing up to pucker brush, stone walls crumbling, homes abandoned, and families splintered as fully forty percent of native-born Vermonters left for other states.

Agriculture, the starting point for the Historical Section's photographs in Vermont, was in crisis. In a state recognized nationally for its rural character, only one third of the population remained on the farm in 1930. Three quarters of these farms had running water, but only a quarter of them had water piped to a bathroom. Two-thirds had telephones, but only one in seven farmers owned a tractor such as Delano found at work in Bellows Falls in 1941. A herd of ten to twelve cows was average; anything larger made a milking machine necessary, but Vermont farms were so widely scattered that electric companies were loathe to invest in the poles and wiring that would have brought light and labor-saving machines into the dark hills. Most farms shipped fluid milk to the Boston market, but a milk surplus depressed prices and meant the average farm operated on a monthly budget of less than fifty dollars.[11] What little leverage Vermont farmers could exert on the market came from their participation in the Grange, the Farm Bureau, and one of the state's thirty-three cooperative creameries. By the 1930s, then, the hallmark Vermonter, but by no means the typical Vermonter, was an overworked, underpaid farmer tied, in many cases, to a marginal farm; compelled by circumstance to labor by hand; restrained by other circumstances from gaining the advantage of new technology; individually powerless in a web of transportation, pricing, and production issues; and too strapped for cash to do anything more than hold on.

The Vermonters who in the 1930s turned to their governments looking for help were infinitely more complex than the images being published of them in books and magazines. Heralded for their conservatism, they defied convention and elected George D. Aiken, a progressive Republican, as governor in 1936. Notwithstanding the fact that they were collecting the highest percentage of federal relief money in New England, they rejected Franklin D. Roosevelt's bid for reelection as president the same year, partly out of fear that his unbalanced budget would throw the country into chaos.[12] So leery of trading their independence for a massive federal government program that they rejected plans for the Green Mountain Parkway, the largest New Deal employment initiative proposed in the state, thousands of Vermonters nevertheless accepted work through the Works Progress Administration, often because they felt they could maintain their pride if they worked for the money instead of accepting handouts. Eventually, the agency sponsored projects in more than half the state's towns.

George Aiken paved the way for the cataclysmic changes of the New Deal. A farmer and horticulturalist from Putney, Aiken entered state politics in 1930 and quickly worked his way up to governor. He was a blunt, plainspoken activist who proved to his skeptical fellow citizens the power of cooperatives and labor unions, introduced Vermonters to new ideas about regulating corporations to serve the public interest, assured Vermonters that meaningful social welfare could be delivered in a dignified way that did not demean them, encouraged Vermonters to protect their natural resources, and generally made them see themselves as part of a large and complex socio-economic unit.[13]

By the time the federal government began launching its New Deal programs in earnest, Vermonters had grown accustomed to having government take an expanded role in their lives. They welcomed WPA teachers into their prisons and WPA musicians and artists into their schools. They recruited young men for the Civilian Conservation Corps and young women as public health nurses. They helped write a state guidebook and conserved historical records. Between 1935 and 1943 they accepted 814,740 garments sewn by the National Youth Administration sewing project for Vermont children on welfare. Vermonters created vocation rehabilitation programs for the disabled, established psychiatric clinics, and accepted unemployment assistance under the Federal Social Security Act.[14]

Even the idea of resettling Vermonters off marginal land was acceptable, because it was not a new idea. In 1928 the Vermont Commission on Country Life organized to study the reasons for the state's decline and to propose ideas that might bring about a rebirth. The commission of two hundred Vermonters studied, among other things, the state's population, resources, industry, heritage, and geography, and its report, published in 1931, made dozens of recommendations about how Vermont could strengthen its economy and society. The most controversial recommendation concerned eugenics and the suggestion that old-stock Yankees should have more children because bloodlines and values were being undermined by poverty and non-Anglo ethnic groups, such as the French Canadian farmers and Spanish granite workers. However, buried within the 385-page report was another controversial recommendation, offered several years ahead of any federal program: that Vermonters abandon trying to cultivate marginal hill farms and relocate to better farms or towns where their chances of rising above their poverty might increase.[15]

Although Vermont had a compelling photographic tradition to draw from, one whose aesthetic and moral stringency were echoed in popular works published to promote the state, books such as *And So Goes Vermont* and *Vermont Beautiful*, what distinguished the Historical Section photographers who made their way into the state beginning in 1936 was that they came with their eyes open. Unlike many of their predecessors, they saw, as if for the first time, everything there was to see. They possessed the natural curiosity that Stryker looked for in the young men and women he hired and nurtured with a missionary's zeal. "He [Stryker] wasn't imposing his idea on you," Jack Delano said in a 1965 interview, "he was trying to get you stimulated enough so that you would find out what was really there."[16]

In other words, although Stryker had his own ideas regarding Vermont, based on his experience in the state, he also gave the photographers who visited Vermont freedom to see the state through their own eyes and not through the eyes and stereotypes of photographers who had come before them. Not surprisingly, they had no trouble finding what others had found. In the Historical Section's file, the beauty of the Vermont landscape is well represented by Arthur Rothstein's, Marion Post's, and Jack Delano's breathtaking photographs; the state's agricultural heritage is evident in Rothstein's stunning photographs of farmers bringing in the hay on a late summer day, and in Rothstein's, Lee's and Delano's pictures of Farm Security Administration clients. The strength of the state's community is evident in everything from Delano's photographs of country fairs to Post's photographs of Woodstock's annual town meeting.

Nor did they have trouble finding what they were told to find. As Stryker inclined them by his insistence that they use one of the editions of Smith's *North America* as their introduction, they looked for and found "in upland Vermont, free from cities," the true, surviving Yankee, "an interesting and sturdy type of man."[17] The wealth of Vermont portraiture that floods the Historical Section's file suggests the extent of their efforts to capture on film the state's human character. These portraits, not just of faces but of stooped backs and weathered hands, are testaments to what Vermont writer Walter Hard has called "hard living in a hard place," spilling beyond stereotypes and opening themselves up to interpretations that did not sentimentalize the oppressive demands of farm life.

Fortunately, the Historical Section's extravagant file also had room in it for important photographs that had never before been taken, the kind that were more a warning than a tribute. No one before Carl Mydans had ever made a record of the state's abandoned farms, not with the idea of publicizing them to affluent out-of-staters for summer homes but to bear mute witness to the dashed hopes of generations of disappointed Vermont farmers. Neither had anyone photographed Vermont's middle class, meaning not the pillars of the state's politics and industry—the Fairbanks and the Proctors and other similar family dynasties—nor the stereotypical hill farmer, icon to the nation (and Stryker) of Jeffersonian agrarian ideals. Rather, here were typical Vermonters, Rotarians, salesmen, businessmen, housewives, fairgoers, and ordinary voting citizens. Finally, no one had gone into homes, as Russell Lee did, to take wrenching photographs of families living beyond the fringes, not just economically, but, as is apparent from the interiors, culturally and spiritually as well. These homes may not have been the ones visited by representatives from the Commission on Country Life, but Vermonters such as these almost certainly prompted the commission to address eugenics in its final report. Unlike the commission, Lee responded to the brutal environment with almost tender photographs that evoke enormous sympathy for the state's hidden shame.

In many and surprising ways, the Historical Section's Vermont photographs reinterpreted the state. Vermonters, idealized elsewhere as moral and upright, are captured at the fair clearly enjoying their liquor, the absurd side shows, and the scandalous girlie shows as much as people elsewhere. Delano's photographs of men making paper in Sheldon Springs, their glistening torsos emerging from the steam like damned souls in Hell, suggest both honest, hard labor and the paintings of socialist labor reformer Diego Rivera. Similarly, the dairy cooperative photographs of Delano, Post, and Lee indicate the extent to which the independent Vermont farmer of the 1930s was a fading myth. Pastoral farm scenes, although they are abundant, ultimately give way in these photographs to tractors and milking machines and the realities of contemporary commerce. The town and village scenes are compelling reflections of the complexities of small-town life, but the relatively few urban scenes are equally important because they capture life in some of the few places in Vermont where the population was growing and business was getting on in the face of the depression. Here, and not in the bucolic country scenes that earlier photographers had favored, there was growing critical mass and the industry necessary to carry the state into the future.

The portrait succeeds so brilliantly because of its scope and depth. Stryker knew instinctively that any place is fundamentally unknowable from a single photograph. His photographers continued to try to distill a place in a single photograph, but it was never their boss's intention to reduce any region or place to a solitary image. "I remember sending young Jack Delano on assignment to Vermont," Stryker recalled in 1973 in *In This Proud Land*, the single book he wrote about the photographs taken by the Historical Section and his experience with the program. "He [Delano] spent hours asking himself, a bit self-consciously, 'What is the one picture I can take that will say Vermont?' "[18] That goal eluded

Delano, but his was a magnificent failure, for he supplied more than seven hundred images of the state, almost half of all the Historical Section photographs taken in Vermont, creating an incomparable mosaic of the state on the eve of World War II.

Neither did Stryker expect the photographers who worked for him to go out into the field and take "great" photographs. Some photographs did become cultural icons, combining exquisite aesthetic qualities, technical perfection, and almost overpowering emotional content, but the photographers' assignment was much more basic. Looking back thirty years after the program ended, Stryker wrote, "We succeeded in doing exactly what Rex Tugwell said we should do: We introduced Americans to Americans."[19] Eight Historical Section photographers, plus independent Louise Rosskam, achieved this in Vermont by following Stryker's advice to find the telling detail—the starched, white apron; the child's work boot; the dirty, gnarled hands; the paint flaking from a sleigh in the dooryard; the weather-worn face; the foot on the railing; the field patterned with neat rows of cut hay—and from these details came great, irresistible photographs of incredible complexity and artistry.

Stryker was surprised later in his life to discover how profoundly the photographers of the Historical Section had influenced photography. Ansel Adams called them "a bunch of sociologists with cameras."[20] Walker Evans, whose painterly compositions influenced almost every photographer who followed him at the Historical Section, believed they were artists. Others, including Edwin Rosskam, who claimed to have coined the word, called them photojournalists, but Stryker always bristled at that label. He believed that photographers as journalists were no different from writers and deserved the honor of being called simply journalists. In addition, they were historians, deliberately and self-consciously creating the most complete visual record ever made of one era in American life. Stryker also intended that the Historical Section photographers be teachers. In choosing the two hundred photographs that illustrate *In This Proud Land*, including the six representing Vermont, Stryker selected not just the two or three icons everyone would expect but also those photographs that best illustrated how Americans of the depression era related to each other, their work, their government, and their land.

These are photographs meant to raise questions. Each has its story, to be sure, a small universe framed from an even smaller viewfinder, and an astonishing number of them are complete unto themselves as works of surpassing art, but it is impossible to look at the photographs of Vermont without asking questions such as, Where are the parents? How much longer will farmers be able to scythe a field and stay competitive? What is the length of a man's working life under those conditions? What hope is there for a woman's spirit buried in the work of childrearing and isolated on a hill farm? What is the human cost of that pastoral landscape?

These are fundamentally different questions than any raised before by images of Vermont. In the decades before the Historical Section photographers trained their lenses on the state, images of it raised essentially two questions: Is it the truth? (to which the answer was sometimes no) and Is it admirable? (to which the answer increasingly was a resounding yes). The section photographs prompted the first question again: Is it the truth? Unfortunately, as Americans became painfully aware after experiencing a stream of these photographs from every corner of the country, the answer was yes. More to the point, however, the Historical Section photographs raised a profoundly different and disturbing second question: Is this acceptable?

This moral imperative overlays the section's photographs like a fixative. As much as the technical expertise and artistry, it sets them apart from decades of images of Vermont that came before. That morality derived from Roy Stryker, but he had the wisdom to find and employ men and women who understood the importance of asking the question, Is this acceptable? and who had the artistic skills to express it in ways that continue to command our attention. The photographers of the Historical Section were blessed with an extraordinary ability to see what was before them; their gaze was direct and unflinching. Vermont through their eyes is both comfortingly familiar and shockingly new.

NOTES

1 / *Vermonter* (August 1895): 1.

2 / Nutting, p. ix.

3 / Hogan, in Orton, p. 2.

4 / Fisher, in Federal Writers' Project, p. 3.

5 / Vermont Writers' Project, p. 1.

6 / Millstein, p. 717.

7 / Brault, p. 131.

8 / Smith and Phillips, pp. 7, 10.

9 / Ibid., p. 151.

10 / Judd, p. 8.

11 / Ibid., p. 98.

12 / Ibid., p. 56.

13 / Ibid., p. 207.

14 / Ibid., p. 220.

15 / Two Hundred Vermonters, p. 130.

16 / Delanos interview, pp. 7–8.

17 / Smith and Phillips, p. 150.

18 / Stryker and Wood, p. 8.

19 / Ibid., p. 9.

20 / Ibid., p. 8.

WORKS CITED

All letters cited, unless otherwise noted, are among the *Roy Emerson Stryker Papers, 1932–1964,* available through the Archives of American Art, Smithsonian Institution, Washington, D.C., in an edition edited by David Horvath and microfilmed by Chadwick-Healey, Alexandria, Virginia. In addition, I relied heavily on interviews of most of the photographers conducted by Richard K. Doud. These were recorded and transcribed, and are now part of the Smithsonian Institution's Archives and Manuscripts Catalog. Like the collection of Stryker letters and memorabilia, the transcribed interviews are available in a microfilm edition.

Anderson, Sherwood. *Home Town.* New York: Alliance Book, 1940.

Boatz, Willfried. *Photography: An Illustrated Historical Overview.* Hauppauge [N.Y.]: Barron's, 1997.

Brault, Gerard J. "Photographs of French Canadian Children Working in New England Textile Mills by Lewis W. Hine, 1908–1916." *French Canadian and Acadian Genealogical Review* 8 (1980): 131–140.

"Community Notes." *Randolph Herald and News,* 11 September 1941, p. 4; and 25 September 1941, p. 4.

Crane, Charles Edward. *Let Me Show You Vermont.* New York: Alfred A. Knopf, 1937.

———. *Winter in Vermont.* New York: Alfred A. Knopf, 1941.

Curtis, James. *Mind's Eye, Mind's Truth: FSA Photography Reconsidered.* Philadelphia: Temple University Press, 1989.

Delano, Jack. *Photographic Memories.* Washington: Smithsonian Institution Press, 1997.

Delano, Jack, and Irene Delano. Interview by Richard K. Doud, 12 June 1965. Oral History Collections, Archives of American Art, Smithsonian Institution, Washington, D.C.

Ellis, Arthur. "Camera Angles." *Washington Post,* 21 August 1938.

Federal Writers' Project. *Vermont: A Guide to the Green Mountain State.* Boston: Houghton Mifflin, 1937.

Hurley, F. Jack. *Marion Post Wolcott: A Photographic Journey.* Albuquerque: University of New Mexico Press, 1989.

———. *Portrait of a Decade: Roy Stryker and the Development of Documentary Photography in the Thirties.* Baton Rouge: Louisiana State University, 1972.

Judd, Richard Munson. *The New Deal in Vermont: Its Impact and Aftermath.* New York: Garland Publishing, 1979.

Lee, Russell. "Life on the American Frontier." *U.S. Camera* (October 1941).

———. *Russell Lee: Photographer.* Ed. F. Jack Hurley. Dobbs Ferry, N.Y.: Morgan and Morgan, 1978.

Lee, Russell, and Jean Lee. Interview by Richard K. Doud, 2 June 1964. Oral History Collections, Archives of American Art, Smithsonian Institution, Washington, D.C.

Macmillan Biographical Encyclopedia of Photographic Artists and Innovators. Eds. Turner Browne and Elaine Partnow. New York: Macmillan, 1983.

Millstein, Barbara Head. "Lewis Wickes Hine: The Final Years." *Antiques* (November 1998): 714–721.

Mydans, Carl. *Carl Mydans: Photojournalist.* Interview by Philip B. Kunhardt Jr. New York: Harry N. Abrams, 1985.

Mydans, Carl. Interview by Richard K. Doud, 29 April 1964. Oral History Collections, Archives of American Art, Smithsonian Institution, Washington, D.C.

Nutting, Wallace. *Vermont Beautiful.* Garden City [N.Y.]: Garden City Publishing, 1922.

O'Neal, Hank. *A Vision Shared: A Classic Portrait of America and Its People, 1935–1943.* New York: St. Martin's Press, 1976.

Ormsbee, Charles, and Marilyn Ormsbee Piro. Interview with author, 24 May 1999.

Ormsbee, Myrtle. Personal diary.

Orton, Vrest, ed. *And So Goes Vermont: A Picture Book of Vermont as It Is.* Weston [Vt.]: Countryman Press, 1937.

Photographers Encyclopedie International: 1839 to the Present. Switzerland: Editions Camera Obscura, 1975.

Post Wolcott, Marion. Interview by Richard K. Doud, 18 January 1965. Oral History Collections, Archives of American Art, Smithsonian Institution, Washington, D.C.

Rosskam, Edwin, and Louise Rosskam. Interview by Richard K. Doud, 3 August 1965. Oral History Collections, Archives of American Art, Smithsonian Institution, Washington, D.C.

Rosskam, Louise. Telephone interviews with author, 15 October 2000 and 10 November 2000.

Rothstein, Arthur. Interview by Richard K. Doud, 25 May 1964. Oral History Collections, Archives of American Art, Smithsonian Institution, Washington, D.C.

Severin, Werner Joseph. "Photographic Documentation by the Farm Security Administration, 1935–1942." Master's thesis, School of Journalism, University of Missouri, 1959.

Smith, J. Russell, and Ogden Phillips. *North America: Its People and the Resources, Development and Prospects of the Continent as the Home of Man.* 3d ed. New York: Harcourt Brace, 1942.

Stange, Maren. "Publicity, Husbandry, and Technology: Fact and Symbol in Civilian Conservation Corps Photography." In *Official Images: New Deal Photography.* Washington, D.C.: Smithsonian Institution Press, 1987, 66–91.

———. "The Record Itself: FSA Photography and the Transformation of Rural Life." In *Official Images: New Deal Photography.* Washington, D.C.: Smithsonian Institution Press, 1987, 1–35.

Stryker, Roy Emerson. Interview by Richard K. Doud, 17 October 1963. Oral History Collections, Archives of American Art, Smithsonian Institution, Washington, D.C.

Stryker, Roy Emerson, and Nancy Wood. *In This Proud Land: America 1935–1943 as Seen in the FSA Photographs.* Greenwich [Conn.]: New York Graphic Society, 1973.

Two Hundred Vermonters. *Rural Vermont: A Program for the Future.* Burlington [Vt.]: The Vermont Commission on Rural Life, 1931.

Vachon, John. "Tribute to a Man, an Era, and Art." *Harper's* (September 1973): 96–99.

Vermonter: An Illustrated Monthly Magazine, The. August 1895.

Vermont Writers' Project and the Work Projects Administration for the State of Vermont. *Vermont: A Profile of the Green Mountain State.* Burlington [Vt.]: 1941.

Washington Daily News, 18 December 1935.